Glass Half Full

Our Australian Adventure

By

Sarah Jane Butfield

Dedication

This book is dedicated to Sheila Anne Garratt.

Nigel's mother, Sheila, lost her battle with cancer during our time in Australia.

Her memory and spirit lives on in our hopes and dreams for the future.

Acknowledgments

I would not have been able to write this book without the support of my husband, Nigel, who has worked hard to allow me to be a full-time writer. I would like to thank the many friends and relatives who have read the work in progress to assist me with the development and editing. Special thanks to Sandra Kaiser, John Butfield and Julia James for reading the entire book, giving their honest critique and feedback.

My thanks also go to my children Samantha, Robert, and Jaime, for helping to raise awareness of my book on social media.

Sarah Jane and Nigel Butfield in Alice Springs, Australia 2008
This is our story.

Chapter Index

Chapter 1

What will the children say?

"Why Australia? Why now?" Samantha spluttered, almost choking on her jacket potato and beans, as we announced the topic of that night's family conference.

"That's awesome!" said Robert, a keen surfer.

"Can we have a kangaroo?" said Jaime, eager to show off her knowledge of Australian animals.

This is how it started, our journey, not just the physical one, but also the psychological, social and emotional ones to achieving our dream of a new life in Australia. Our journey would test us in so many ways, and we would have only our positive approach to life to lean on during the toughest times.

Sometimes, enough is enough. In 1997, living or just surviving, I was on the hamster wheel of a life. As a single mum, I juggled a full-time nursing job, with parenting three young children living at home. It was time for something to change. For many years, had behaved like a victim, allowing myself to wallow in self-pity and the 'why me?' syndrome. My glass appeared half-empty, with no refill accessible. The breakdown of my first marriage was to a man eleven years my senior. My second marriage, dubbed 'The Sham,' was to a prolific philanderer. When it ended, a wound was torn in my heart when, despite him refusing to divorce me, the court awarded custody of my beautiful baby daughter Molly to him.

I tried to find a sense of family, after my mum died, but this ended in a fruitless search for my biological father. I used the divorces, the custody battle and my mum's death as excuses for my tolerance of undeserving people, despite intuitively knowing that my life did not have to be this way. Changes, in whatever form I made them, had to ensure that from then on I would always see my glass as half-full. I

1

decided not to squander my time on undeserving people, or those who did not appreciate the value of life itself. This new positive approach would help me perceive my glass as half-full and achieve a good life for myself and my children.

In 1997, I met Nigel; we live life to the full. We have no children together, but I have four children, Samantha and Robert from my first marriage, and Molly and Jaime from my second. Nigel has three children, Laurence, Phillip and Clair, so together we have made our contribution to the population. Family life for us has always been busy yet fun. At any one time, three or four of the children lived with us, and the others visited on weekends and during the school holidays.

From left to right: Sarah Jane, Phillip, Jaime, Clair, Robert, Samantha, Sheila and Nigel at the front.

In 2007, two of our children had recently moved out of the family home. Robert, seventeen years old, was living and working on a holiday resort complex in the seaside town of Looe, Cornwall, UK. Samantha, nineteen years old also worked there, and she lived with her partner Doug, in nearby Liskeard. Despite living away from home, they always returned once a week for dinner and they never missed a family conference. We always used family conferences around the dinner table, to discuss important matters like moving house, or changing jobs or schools. On this occasion, we decided that, in addition to the family conferences, we also needed one-to-one talks with each of them. That way they were free to have their say, un-influenced by their siblings.

These hard discussions took time and patience, but we are very proud of the mature way in which they listened, questioned, accepted and understood our rationale for moving to Australia. As you can imagine, finding the right time to consider an international move was never going to be easy. In addition, Nigel and I struggled with my problematic ex-husband, Jack, Jaime's biological father, from day one of our relationship, mainly in relation to child custody issues. .Hence this would become one of the biggest hurdles to overcome in order to start our new adventure 'down under'.

In February 2007, with only one child, Jaime, living at home permanently, we made our first visit to Australia. We visited Nigel's father John, who lives in the state of Tasmania. John emigrated ten years ago to become a caregiver for his widowed mother whose health was deteriorating. At that time, John was divorced from Nigel's mother, Sheila, but after ten years apart, they were back in touch and trying to reconcile their relationship. We immediately felt at home in Australia, falling in love with the dream of a more fulfilling life. The substantial career opportunities and a life-changing experience for us all drifted into our viewfinder. There would be increased opportunity for the outdoor activities we love as a family, camping, walking and beach holidays. All we had to decide was, whether it was the right time and the right thing to do, for our family and for us.

Decision made on our part: we wanted to go. During our stay, we visited not only Hobart in Tasmania, but also Sydney in New South Wales and Alice Springs in the Northern Territory. We saw and experienced a cross-section of outback, metropolitan and regional

Australia in two states and one territory. February is summertime in Australia. The temperatures and humidity vary considerably from state to state. With temperatures of 20°C and changeable in Hobart, 28°C and balmy in Sydney, and 40°C and arid in Alice Springs we had it all. We realised, soon, after the initial research, that if we wanted to pursue a new life in Australia we would have to apply before my forty-fifth birthday. If not, then we would have no chance of an employer sponsored visa, based on my nursing experience and qualifications. The ideal scenario would be to achieve the move before Jaime started high school. Therefore, we had a quite a small window of opportunity to make our dream a reality. The decision to move to another country is a process. The decision involves not only the formal process, but also the moral and personal decision-making process. This requires the input of the whole family to ensure success. There are no hard-and-fast rules that apply to making the 'right' decision, and there will always be an element of compromise on someone's part.

So, back to the children. Samantha, Robert, and Jaime had been at our first family conference, and although Samantha was shocked at our decision, she understood our rationale. However, she knew her partner Doug would never leave the UK. If we went then she would have to choose between coming with us and staying with Doug. Robert would be eighteen years old by the time we left. We knew he would jump at this opportunity, as a keen traveller and an avid, experienced surfer. Robert, having surfed at various Cornish coastal towns, for most of his teenage years, was eager to go to the Mecca for all surfers.

The first big question was what the other children would say. For Laurence, Clair, Phillip and Molly, who were not moving with us, we focused entirely on the contact visits and communication methods. Laurence, Clair and Phillip were living in Colchester with their mother, Tracey, Nigel's ex-wife. Molly was living with Jack, who over the years had refused me contact with her when it suited his circumstances, though he had never shown any interest in Jaime. We knew this would change when he became aware of our plans, and it did. We were adamant that, given the challenges of the process, the discussions about contact frequency and methods of communication should be based on honesty and facts, not pipedreams through rose-tinted spectacles.

However, the most important question was, how would we all cope with the reality of being separated by continents? With our tangled web of family relationships to consider, we had our work cut out. The result of our family conferences and one-to-one discussions was that Jaime and Robert wanted to come to Australia with us. We needed court approval for Jaime because, unsurprisingly, Jack lodged an order to prevent the move and a custody request for her. Guilt is a reasonably small word, but one which has such a huge impact. We rode a wave of guilty thoughts and feelings, as we discussed, researched, and investigated if we could actually make the move happen, and if we could live with the consequences.

The Australian visa process and criteria were very stringent, and highly scrutinized. As we talked and interacted with people living and working in Alice Springs, both in person and afterwards by email, it was evident that there was a high demand for skilled professionals in all fields of healthcare. In the Northern Territory, for all areas of healthcare services, the process can be faster and the packages of relocation and salary benefits more lucrative. Therefore, although Alice Springs was not our ideal destination, we knew that we could use the system to help us achieve our dream. In exchange for two years in Alice Springs, taking advantage of the benefits of territory tax allowances, extra annual leave, parental leave, etc., we could relocate anywhere in Australia. At the end of my contract, with permanent residency in place, Australia and all its wonders would be open to us. Our preferred destination to live in was Queensland, near to the Sunshine and Gold Coasts, bordering Brisbane. This would enable easy access to the beaches, snorkelling, whale watching, and the outdoor lifestyle we wanted for not only ourselves but for our children. We wanted to create a family home, that any of the children could come to, and call home.

A work offer at the Alice Springs Hospital was quickly and efficiently sourced and processed. After an internet search for nursing vacancies in Alice Springs, I found a variety of positions available, with great scope for career progression. I completed an online application form, had my criminal reference bureau police check completed in the UK, and Alice Springs Hospital checked my professional references. A self-assessment professional development questionnaire and telephone interview followed. I had to take a medication-calculation test that landed, because of the time difference between the UK and Australia, in the small hours of the morning. I feared my tiredness might jeopardise the results, but my worries were ill-founded. I completed it successfully and we had the first piece of the visa criteria in place. The result was an offer of employment with a two-year contract. This was subject to acceptance onto the Australian Nurse Register. The contract came with sponsorship for a skilled entry 457 temporary visa initially, with the ability to apply for a permanent resident skilled entry 857 sponsored visa after a three-month probationary period.

The next step of the visa process was to obtain recognition and accreditation of my nursing qualifications from the Northern Territory Nursing Board and ANMC – Australian Nursing and Midwifery Council. This was a lengthy and bureaucratic process, but obviously very necessary when employing a healthcare professional who has been trained overseas. I sourced the transcripts of my nurse-training syllabus and results, obtaining them from the archives at Anglia Ruskin University, in Chelmsford. The submission of certified copies of my nursing qualifications and professional development certificates followed, and after the payment of the registration fees, the wait began. When my Australian Nurse Registration certificate arrived, we were another step closer to achieving our dream. Our visa application was submission-ready, subject to the court granting permission for Jaime to move to Australia. Sadly, as anticipated, this permission was not forthcoming from her biological father, Jack. He lodged a custody application, which the court denied because of the lack of an existing relationship between him and Jaime. Nevertheless, pending reports and a final hearing, a contact order was granted to him for supervised visits with Jaime in a contact centre in Cornwall. The stress for me of just being in the same room as him was bad enough. For Jaime, spending time with this virtual stranger, whose body language demonstrated no love for her, was especially stressful.

So, let the battles of this war of commence; enter the solicitors, barristers and social workers.

Chapter 2

What have we got ourselves into now?

In my experience, the child custody and court procedures, generally favour the manipulators. I played by the rules and failed to win custody of my daughter Molly. They favoured a stay-at-home, dole scrounger like my ex-husband, Jack, over a full-time, working mum already successfully raising two children.

I continually and consciously remind myself during life's testing and difficult times: I am going to survive this, I am a good person, and I deserve to be happy. I value life. The death of my mum in her fifties, before she saw or experienced her grandchildren, reinforced the fact that there are no guarantees about life expectancy. Therefore, I want to make the most of every minute, of every day of my life. I strive to ensure that I surround everyone around me with positive thoughts and actions. I am a true believer in 'what goes around comes around.' If you always treat others the way you would like to be treated, then you will attract positivity from the people and experiences you encounter. Unfortunately, not everyone who has entered my life has shared my viewpoint. I have been hurt, physically and emotionally, on many levels in my life to date. Despite this, I have always tried to instil my positivity in my family's capabilities. This, I hope, equips them to overcome the many challenges and uncertainties faced as individuals and as a family.

I was motivated to interact with other people who were also failed by the system or enduring similar experiences. Nigel and I joined an online British expat forum to help us research and manage the immigration process. Despite the stress and expense of our year-long child custody proceedings, my soul was nurtured through sharing experiences on the forum. The camaraderie, advice, and support from the members we encountered was immeasurably helpful. It impacted not only the child custody and permission process, but also visa choice and application aspects. The assistance of the moderators and migration agents is a valuable asset, and we offer our greatest thanks to all involved. Everyone wants to read the good news stories, but when you are in the midst of the child custody system, you feel compelled to read the sad news stories too. These people need the support of others with experience of the process. Heroically, some of them, despite their own sorrow, were still willing to advise and assist those of us still working in the maze of social worker assessments, contact centre visits etc. We gleaned precious fragments of advice, shared on the forum, from those successful in gaining permission as well as those refused the right to remove their child. The sadness and heartache witnessed, when reading news of a failed request to relocate or an unsuccessful custody hearing, still haunts me now.

The year-long children's court battle subjected our family to extreme, enduring, bureaucratic scrutiny. This tested our commitment to pursue our dream. The accusations, innuendo, and interrogation of our character and our lives commenced and continued, unrelenting. The court assigned us a Family Court Adviser (FCA) from an independent organisation known as the Children and Family Court Advisory and Support Service. (CAFCASS) The role of the FCA is to gather information about what would be in the 'best interests' of the child and report to the court with their findings and recommendations. The other role, in our case, involved facilitating mediation and supervised contact visits. As parents or just as human beings, you can probably imagine the hurt we suffered. We had been parents for over twenty years, raising healthy, well-adjusted and intelligent children, so having a social worker interview you to discuss your methods feels insulting, most certainly so when it is implied we were inflicting the stress on our children. It sickens me still that anyone might doubt our ability to provide the best care and upbringing for Jaime, or any of our children. For Nigel, this intrusive process provoked a unique mixture of emotions. Over the years, he had witnessed the effects of Jack on not only my life, but on the lives of our other children. He hated Jack for it. Nigel is a very straight-talking person and as the only 'daddy' Jaime ever knew, this intrusion was offensive. When Jaime's session involved carrying out role-play by placing stones on a mat, I sensed Nigel's anger. The stones represented members of her family whom she loved, cared about and would miss. There was stone for Jack and a stone for Nigel, but when Jack's was designated the 'daddy' stone, it broke Nigel's heart. Our ability as parents was put to the test in ways I hope few ever have to endure. Our whole life laid bare for social workers, solicitors, teachers and Jack to see.

Unlike my second husband, who has a colourful criminal record, my only court experience in the past had been the children's court proceedings during my custody battles for Molly. His confidence in the courtroom added to my overwhelming feelings of anxiety and torment. So much was at stake. The possibility of losing another daughter to this man and letting him destroy me again weighed heavy on my heart. In the past, Samantha and Robert had endured the side effects of my relentless efforts to have contact and build a relationship with my daughter Molly. They watched me do anything and everything, including degrading myself in a failed attempt at reconciling the sham of a marriage, during which I became pregnant with Jaime.

On each occasion, during this new battle, we had to sit in the child custody court behind solicitors, barristers and court officials unable to respond. We would listen to accusations and reports on every aspect of our life as it was probed in minute detail, including our parenting skills, our relationship and most importantly our parental decision-making. They criticised, examined and scrutinized us, the couple, cast as the villains of this drama. We endured his solicitor's intimation of our disrespect for Jack, as we attempted to separate a 'father' from access to this daughter. The process made me feel like a criminal; I felt more as if the judge would pass sentence rather than award custody. I would sit there wringing my hands together until pain alerted me to the act. I would be physically shaking, despite Nigel's arm around me, so tight that his fingers pressed into the skin of my arm through a jumper and a coat. Cold to the core, as if hypothermic, I had to question many times if it was worth the pain and torment. I had vowed never to let him into my life again and yet we were in the same room. My skin crawled with feelings of loathing, and honestly, hatred surged through me. He had deprived me of the mother/daughter relationship with Molly, and wanted nothing to do with Jaime, until she became a pawn in a game. Jack revelled in the power he had and he believed that he would stop us from leaving the UK. Jack had taken us down a horrible path and we had jumped through the hoops like loyal sheepdogs.

On the day of the final hearing, as we sat in the court interview rooms with our barrister, she broke the awkward silence as she shuffled her paperwork. "If I were his representation today, I would be more than a little annoyed at his tardiness."

She was obviously referring to the fact that Jack was leaving it very late to arrive. I remember Nigel looking at me in the briefing room, in that split second knowing that we were both thinking the same thing. Was this another of his games to delay the process, or had he come up with another obstacle to put in our way? Despite reassurances from our barrister, our mood was sombre. We held hands under the table, like clinging to each other on a cliff edge. The only lifeline our positive thinking; we would get the decision for which we had prayed. The psychological agony we endured during this wait is still hard to think about and describe. I hated the thought of seeing Jack, or even hearing his name, but on this occasion, we were waiting for him. We needed him to arrive, to bring this episode of hurt, distress and anxiety to an end. Not knowing if the court would rule in our favour, we were too numb from the interrogatory process to speculate. Hope was all we had, and the desire to be able to extricate ourselves after being dragged once again into his unscrupulous world.

Jack must have known or been advised that he would be unsuccessful, because he did not bother to attend. Instead, our barrister received a call from his solicitor asking to postpone or if the judge ruled against that, we were to proceed without him. He claimed to have been involved in a car crash the previous evening, and that due to whiplash he could not attend. Based on his previous excuses, to delay or for non-attendance at mediation sessions, we recognised its dishonest intent. However, putting aside the feelings of anger and annoyance at his manipulation, the relief at being told that the hearing would still be going ahead brought some respite.

Sarah Jane Butfield

The decision announcement came in a jumble of words: I did not know if I fully understood the conclusion. The barristers started debating the finer details of the order which the judge would sign and approve that day. It smacked of watching a reality television show, events and words bandied about and happening around me, but I could not do anything to interact with them. I think the shock, combined with the relief that this ordeal was over, hit me in an all-consuming manner. I do not remember if I responded to the announcement of the decision. When we came out of the courtroom, I clung to Nigel with every ounce of strength left in me. In reality, he was holding me up.

A mixture of feelings swam through my head, the most pressing of which being the fear that I had misunderstood the decision. This annoying fear hovered over me, buzzing in my brain, like mosquitoes over a stagnant pond until the barrister walked out. She came from behind us with the court order in her hand. As I glimpsed the red official stamp in the approval section, I knew it was over and she held our ticket to a new life.

After dragging our family, but more importantly Jaime, through this intrusive and degrading process he failed to pull us apart. Inadvertently, he had made us stronger, as a family unit and as a couple. We could now make our dream a reality. I will never forget seeing the tears in Nigel's, and his mum's eyes when we came home to her and Jaime. To see Nigel giving her the news of the court's approval, for Jaime to leave the UK brought relief and joy. It revealed itself in the form of copious tears and smiles. A prolonged, family embrace released the pent- up emotions of the last year: an amazing and touching moment.

With the permission granted for Jaime to leave the UK, we hurried to the library near the court to scan the court order to our immigration case officer. The wait for a reply was akin to waiting for judgement day. Due to the time difference, we would sit in bed with the laptop on, refreshing the visa-tracking screen, waiting to see the visa approved status appear. At last, we saw what we had been waiting for, 'visa approved.' The email arrived just minutes later; confirmation of an approved visa on the 10th January 2008. Ready, with everything planned after receiving the court permission, and now with our visa approval, we booked our flights for 18th January, 2008. This allowed us time to see the children for our tearful goodbyes. To pack and prepare we went to stay with Sheila, Nigel's mum, for our last few days in the UK.

My two-year contract at Alice Springs Hospital as Registered General Nurse on the medical ward would begin at the end of January. At last, after a harrowing year of court appearances, social work assessments and visa processing our jigsaw puzzle of pieces forming the picture of our future in Australia was complete.

Our dream was finally a reality: let our new life begin.

Chapter 3
Pommes arriving in the desert

There has always been controversy over the true origin of the term 'Pomme.' In Australia, however you choose to say or spell it, pom, pomme or pommey means 'anyone from the UK'. The *Oxford dictionary* states that there is 'no firm evidence for the pomegranate theory,' as first described by D H Lawrence in 1923. However, contradicting this there is a book called 'Kangaroo,' with a paragraph that says, 'Pommy,' is supposed to be short for pomegranate. Pomegranate, invariably pronounced 'Pommygranate,' sounds like a rhyme, in a country with a naturally rhyming dialect. Furthermore, immigrants were recognised during their first months, before their blood 'thins down,' by their round and ruddy cheeks. The pomegranate theory, accepted by the majority as the true origin is in *The Anzac Book* of 1916. Australians and Europeans alike claim another possible origin; that it is an abbreviation for Prisoner Of Her Majesty. (POM) This is related to the convict ships' inhabitants arriving in Australia, although some say it is short for Port of Melbourne, where the convict ships docked.

In Alice Springs, outback Australians use the word 'pomme' frequently, although I doubt many have ever given consideration as to its origin. However, you still occasionally find it used in a derogatory sense. Alice Springs, originally named 'Stuart,' or 'The Springs,' is in the geographical centre of Australia. The settlement around this new telegraph station was renamed Alice Springs after Lady Alice Todd, the wife of Sir Charles Todd, Postmaster General of South Australia. In 1872 they named the Todd River, which flows through Alice Springs, after Sir Charles Todd.

As a remote town in the Northern Territory, it is also famous as the 'Heart of Australia', or 'The Red Centre'. Notable by its dramatic physical appearance, Alice Springs is dry, dusty, red, and arid the majority of the time, in brazen contrast to the deep blue skies which are predominantly cloud free. The earth and surrounding rocky hills are varying shades of red and orange, which reflect the sun's intense rays and cast irregular-shaped shadows onto the paths and roads. In the late afternoon these shadows can be unnerving, as they can resemble large scary faces worthy of inclusion in a Stephen King movie.

The normally dry Todd River in flow Alice Springs 2010

It is rare to see the Todd River flow with water, but we saw it twice during our time in Alice Springs. The riverbed weaves its way through the town, strewn with random dried-out branches, fallen gum trees, bushes, and VB (Victoria bitter) beer cans. Localised groups of indigenous aboriginal residents sit around smoking, drinking and sometimes fighting. I remember the advice Teresa gave me: encourage Jaime to look away from the riverbed as we pass. It is common to see 'kungas,' adult aboriginal women, lifting their skirts to urinate or defecate in open view; they often wear no underwear.

Alice Springs is a unique experience for individuals and families from overseas. Aside from the impact of an international move, there is a period of adjustment to the cultural differences. Also the physical location of Alice Springs presented its own difficulties. Alice Springs can, and does feel isolated from the rest of Australia, especially in challenging times, despite the transport links available. The journey from the UK to reach 'The Alice,' as the local inhabitants refer to it, starts with an international flight. London Heathrow Airport flights go to any one of Australia's international airports, for example, Melbourne, Sydney, Perth, Brisbane or Darwin. A connecting internal domestic flight of approximately two and a half to three hours, will deliver you directly into Alice Springs Airport.

We organised flights into Perth, Western Australia; the most economical route for a family in January 2008. As we were entering Australia on a sponsored work visa, the relocation package on offer helped us a great deal. Even though this only covered internal domestic flight reimbursement, after the costs involved in the visa process and the court proceedings, our priority was cost containment. We landed at Perth International Airport at 2:30 in the morning. We exited the building through the automatic doors and experienced an astounding outside temperature of 25°C. The humidity hit us immediately we stepped outside. The palm trees rustled in the balmy breeze, like arriving at a holiday destination, but we were arriving in our new home, Australia. I remember looking at myself in the unforgiving mirror of the airport shower room as I freshened up from the flight, recalling the reason for my snivelling appearance. My eyes were puffy, like rising bread dough, not only from the flight, but also from the amount of crying on the coach from Liskeard to Heathrow.

Our goodbyes to the children in the run up to our final departure were hard, with tears flowing on each occasion. However, to say goodbye to Samantha at the National Express coach stop in Barras Street, Liskeard, surpassed all expectations: extremely hard is an understatement. Dark, rainy, gloomy - the location mirrored my heart. I thought I had prepared myself for this. How wrong I was! In hindsight, I do not think you can prepare enough. Even though this was a move of our choice, I would miss her immensely. Our relationship was not only that of mother and daughter, but also we were the best and closest of friends.

Although not wanting to show it, Robert struggled to hide his emotions as he said goodbye to his big sister that night. His teenage masculine bravado in the run up to leaving began to wash away with the rain that night. He fought valiantly to hold back his tears. A new void opened for me and Samantha the moment she released from our last embrace. As she turned and hugged her little brother for one last time my heart was breaking.

Robert and Samantha

We boarded the coach with my unrelenting tears streaming down my face. As I attempted to handle the coach tickets, my hand luggage and regain some form of composure in front of Robert and Jaime it soon became clear that it was a futile task.

Once inside the dimly-lit coach, Robert pulled his hoodie up over his face. In the reflection of the coach window Nigel noticed his tears. As he prodded me it pulled me out of my self-pity and back into mother mode, ready to comfort my little boy as he experienced loss for the first time in his life. My heartache from the emotional turmoil of the last few months intensified as I witnessed the pain Robert now endured due to my culpable actions. I knew that they would miss one another more than either of them had anticipated. They have a strong sibling bond, despite their normal teenage squabbles. As they were growing up, Samantha acted like a deputy mother, making sure he was alright and ensuring that I knew if he wasn't. Our close-knit bond of a single parent family in the early years grew from circumstance. After going through so much together in the past, our safety blanket had been having each other to rely on.

Revived temporarily by my shower I stayed with our suitcases so that we did not spark a security incident as the others took their turn in the restrooms. We took advantage of being able to walk around, stretching our legs after the twenty-four-hour long haul flight from London Heathrow via Singapore. We had nearly five hours before our connecting flight to Alice Springs in the morning. The time passed quickly. Our jet lag-induced periods of dozing consumed us as we found a variety of positions to sleep in the airport seating areas. Although not the most comfortable place to sleep, the fact that the seats were empty enabled all of us to lie down and stretch out after the confines of economy class seats

Our flight into Alice Springs seemed short-lived compared to the previous legs of our journey. When you arrive at Alice Springs Airport, you disembark and walk across the tarmac runway from which the heat radiates and instantly feels as if it is burning your feet and legs. The incessant flies, a less favourable feature of life in Alice Springs, invade your eyes, ears, nose and mouth as you momentarily struggle for breath against the dry heat, in contrast to the cool regulated air of the aircraft. The temperature in excess of 40°C came as a shock, even though we had visited Alice Springs before and experienced the flies and heat. I think the combination of jet lag, relief and excitement at starting our new life made the act of breathing and walking to the arrivals areas laboured, but exhilarating all at the same time.

Teresa, Nigel's cousin and her husband Paul and their two children, Abigail and Lauren, met us. The girls had made 'welcome to Australia' signs, which for some reason resurrected my tears when I saw them and they hugged me. I was missing the children already and not for the first time in our journey I had to question again, 'why'?

As if moving to an area of desert in the centre of Australia is not extreme enough, moving to live amongst an indigenous population is a unique experience. No amount of information, research or preparation can equip you for what you will see, hear and experience. It came in stark contrast to a peaceful, seaside town in Cornwall with lush green countryside and clean well-maintained beaches: the immediate differences are obvious. To be honest, it was a strangely breath-taking change, and I wanted to savour everything new surrounding me.

In the airport car park, Nigel and Paul loaded our suitcases and bags into the two cars before we excitedly set off towards our new home. The forty-minute car journey would give us the opportunity to pause and take in the scenery of our new hometown. This being Robert's first visit to Alice Springs, he was noticeably unimpressed. The dry heat and flies irritated his already tired eyes and although he had read the information on Alice Springs in preparation for what he might see, he was obviously shocked. The only redeeming feature for him was it being temporary. Within a week or so, he would be on his way to the coast to pursue his travelling adventures, and of course indulging in his greatest passion, surfing.

Paul, Teresa, Abigail and Lauren.

The houses in Alice Springs tend to be larger than in other Australian states. There are also tight building controls that limit the numbers of two-storey houses permitted. Due to the comparatively large blocks or plots on which they build houses, the tendency to sprawl to absorb the area is commonplace. I recall thinking that some of them resembled sheds or industrial buildings in the UK, because of the steel and corrugated roofing used in their construction. The air-conditioned drive from the airport was a welcome reprieve from the heat.

The lush, green-grassed ovals at sporting arenas and schools stood in stark contrast to the sandy, red paths and gardens of that side of the town. Ironically, in a country where most states are on constant water conservation initiatives, with restrictions widely advertised and enforced, Alice Springs obtains its water from natural underground sources and no such restrictions apply. Despite this, only public places, government buildings and keen gardeners have their sprinkler systems on.

As we turned into Gap Road, I scanned the street's buildings and road signs with my lethargic, heavy eyes looking for the hospital as we drove by. As we passed sports clubs, bars, hotels, holiday apartments, a few residential houses and the aboriginal centres, I wondered where a major hospital would sit in such a built-up area. Then I spotted the big 'H' sign and looked to my left, and there stood Alice Springs Hospital. First impressions; it was smaller than I imagined and it looked similar to a cottage hospital in the UK.

"Here we are," Teresa announced, before I could examine the hospital grounds any further. We pulled up to the gates of the complex, which would be our new home, immediately opposite the hospital.

Nudging Robert, who was dozing again, I said, "That's convenient. No more long commutes for me."

Nigel and I walked over to the hospital main entrance to collect our keys, leaving everyone else in the visitor parking bays. Efficiently the keys were waiting as promised at the enquiries desk, with information on the house, when I needed to sign on and a map of Alice Springs. This was a good start; you need easy when you arrive in the desert with jet lag.

Returning to the cars, we drove into the residents' private parking bays, unloaded our luggage and made our way, searching the doors for number 21. We looked up in awe at the large palm trees gently swaying above the balconies, providing some welcome shade on the path as we walked beside the perfectly manicured borders. The two-bedroomed, air-conditioned townhouse with upstairs balcony was simply styled, with an open plan ground floor area consisting of a fully fitted kitchen, and a lounge/diner. The layout and appearance of space were impressive in such a small house; it would be perfect for us.

To the rear, accessed from the kitchen, was an enclosed courtyard garden with a small grass area, adequate space for a barbecue, table and four chairs. By Australian standards, this house was small, yet compared to traditional English properties it was spacious. In Cornwall, the houses we lived in had small rooms and low ceilings, so the white tiled floors and floor-to-ceiling windows gave our new Australian home a sense of space and light. A great start to our new life.

Robert was only going to be staying with us for a week before moving on to Queensland to be closer to the surf, so he would have the sofa bed downstairs. Therefore, Jaime would have her own bedroom, something that had been a rarity in the UK coming from a large family. Her new bedroom overlooked the courtyard garden. Our bedroom, which had a balcony accessed by double patio doors, had shade-cloth covering and palm trees for shade. Once again, we had to remind ourselves that this was not a holiday destination; this was now our home.

Paul and Teresa left us a pre-cooked meal, and some additional food and drink. We organised times for a shopping trip the next day which left us able to spend the rest of the day settling in, sleeping and trying to work out the air conditioning. In the UK, the only air conditioner we had ever used was in the car, so to see a 'swampie' as Paul called it, was a very new experience.

Swampies consist of a large fan, which propels air over the filters, which are damp, with water from a plumbed supply. With ducting taking the cooled air to all the rooms in the house for our small town house this was more than adequate. Swampies are energy efficient because the fan is the sole moving part, but do not work well when humidity is high. Nigel, always keen to have everything on the perfect setting, made it his mission to achieve a comfortable temperature for our tired bodies and minds to relax in.

We had one day to settle in before I was due to attend my 'sign on' day at the Alice Springs Hospital. We spent our first day walking into the Central Business District (CBD) about twenty minutes away to get some basic food shopping. The two major food supermarkets are Woolworth and Coles. Unlike the UK, you cannot buy alcohol in supermarkets, so there are separate 'bottle shops.' In Alice Springs, which is renowned for its alcohol issues - particularly amongst the indigenous community - there are strict restrictions on when alcohol can be sold and everyone is required to produce identification when making a purchase; something, which irritates a lot of tourists visiting the town.

In January, the height of summer in Australia, the daytime temperature in Alice Springs sits in the mid-forties and you quickly learn not to go out without a bottle of water. The intensity of the heat zaps your strength and even a short walk can feel like a five-kilometre run. Even though Nigel and I love the heat and sunshine, we too struggled with even minor exertion in the early days. However, we adapted more quickly than Robert and Jaime, who needed constant reminders to keep up their fluid intake and utilise the shade when possible.

Sign on day at Alice Springs Hospital

Even though I have been a nurse for over two decades, I still felt nervous and slightly apprehensive as I went to complete the sign on procedure in the Alice Springs Hospital recruitment centre, located at the side of the hospital. I passed an assembly of outbuildings en route containing the nursing library, the hospital laundry and nurses' quarters. The recruitment centre was a small set of three rooms, two offices and a meeting area. All simply and professionally furnished yet humanised with photographs of family and pets on display around the computer screens. I felt like a child starting a new school. I had to get this nervousness in check because this was not even nursing; merely completing the paperwork to be paid my salary.

I do not know why I was surprised, but I noticed immediately that we were all overseas nurses. As we presented our documentation, signed copious forms to set up superannuation and salary sacrificing, we chatted about where we came from and how we came to be in Alice Springs. The stories varied, but with one main theme: Alice Springs was the best destination for a fast, efficient sponsored visa, and for employment due to the high turnover over of its transitional workforce.

Blissfully unaware at this stage of the realities of living in an outback town, I was more than willing to sign up for a two-year minimum contract. When I look back, I realise now why so many people do not make it to the end of their contract and some end up leaving Australia straight from Alice Springs without being able to experience any other States or work places. Therefore, with my contract signed, my hospital scrubs uniforms in hand, name badge printed, security tag and lanyard in place, I was now ready for work.

I was so fortunate to sign on with an enrolled nurse midwife, Carol, originally from Scotland, who unusually had already spent a couple of years in Sydney before arriving here. Carol had moved here with her partner, who was taking up a teaching position at the prestigious St Phillips College. Alice Springs is renowned for its high salaries, generous benefit schedules and promotion opportunities and is therefore a great place for people who are prepared to work hard, earn well and gain experience. Carol became, and still is, my closest friend. It was an amazing experience to complete two years together sharing our highs, and lows, in what would otherwise have been a very lonely town.

Nigel had a wealth of experience from a variety of jobs in the UK, including work as a security guard, taxi driver, second chef in a country hotel restaurant, and his most important job in the early years of our relationship had been house-husband and primary caregiver for

Samantha, Robert and Jaime as I worked full time. The move to Australia meant that Nigel could refocus and rebuild his own career in security, using his experienced and skills. After completing a lot of research into potential work options before we left the UK, Nigel decided to wait and look for work when we arrived. That way he could go and meet people face to face, and more easily obtain the necessary Australian licensing documentation. Despite his low self-confidence, after years as a house-husband and working in non-security related positions, he found employment within three weeks and was quickly promoted to supervisor status. His return to security work would act as a springboard facilitating him becoming a prison officer in 2009, a job he always wanted in the UK, but could never achieve.

Chapter 4
Outback nursing

The Alice Springs Hospital is a 189-bed, specialist teaching hospital. The population that it provides healthcare services for covers over 1.6 million square kilometres, and this scattered distribution of the population provides exceptional and fulfilling challenges in the provision of wide-ranging healthcare services. Some of the services provided include Day Procedures, Accident and Emergency, Intensive Care and High Dependency, Maternity, Medical, Outpatients, Paediatric, Special Care Nursery, Surgical and Mental Health, plus a range of specialist clinical support services.

I have been a Registered General Nurse since 1987, and I have worked in many and varied healthcare environments over the years. Therefore, I thought that I had ample experience to work within a general hospital medical ward. I was wrong. Nursing is supposedly standard across the world. Sick or injured people go to hospital, receive high quality medical care and assistance to regain health or to treat the disease process. In Alice Springs, with an above-average percentage of indigenous people, who have not only mainstream healthcare issues, there are some unique ones as well. Unfortunately, some of them are self-inflicted by cultural and lifestyle choices.

The reluctance of some indigenous individuals to adhere to medical advice and to 'Take their Own Leave,' (TOL) during hospital treatment, makes administering medical attention difficult to say the least. It can be demoralising and frustrating when you strive for the best results, but your efforts are thwarted.

The Alice Springs Hospital education department is fully aware of the detrimental impact that some indigenous peoples responses to health care has on staff morale. This comes from their wealth of experience, over the years, of employing transient workers and experiencing these issues at Alice Springs Hospital (ASH). With this in mind the induction and orientation program for all staff at ASH, is in-depth, thorough and has a huge focus on dealing with the cultural differences of caring for an aboriginal indigenous population.

The government is also fully aware of the wide-ranging healthcare provision issues that exist in the Northern Territory, especially in Alice Springs. Therefore they provide vast amounts of financial resources and funding into the local facilities and organisations that assist with preventative medicine, children's health and alcohol dependency. Despite this, the abuse of the healthcare system continues by some members of the community. It can appear, to non-residents, who literally look in from the periphery and who have not experienced first-hand the genuinely needy indigenous people, that there is little hope for the future of the indigenous population or Alice Springs as a community.

I feel very privileged to have had the opportunity to work in Alice Springs Hospital. The enthusiasm for quality and excellence in all areas is infectious. My experience of nursing in Alice Springs was rewarding, educational and at times highly entertaining. I have no regrets for the choices I made in relation to my career there. I managed to rebuild my acute care nursing confidence, which I admit was low, as in the years leading up to moving to Australia I had worked principally in practice nursing and aged care. I had the experience and the knowledge, however I had not practiced 'hands on' in the acute care environment for a few years, and things change a great deal in a short space of time in healthcare. In exchange for the opportunity to help enhance my skill base on a practical level, I imparted the benefit of my years of nurse management and nurse education experience, thus adding value to the roles I fulfilled during my two years working at Alice Springs Hospital. I was fortunate to meet and work with some truly inspirational and highly experienced nurses on the medical ward.

When I think back to my first shift, which was nerve racking, I still find it hard to believe that I put myself, a woman in her forties, in such a position. What was I thinking? It was like being a newly qualified nurse all over again. I sat in the staff room, which doubled as the hand-over room, surrounded by other staff in their hospital scrubs not knowing what to expect. The problem with scrubs as uniforms is that you can't tell what grade or qualification anyone is, until you get up close to their ID badge. I could have been in a room full of janitors for all I knew. Both sides of the A4 sized handover sheet, featured details of the patients on the sixty-bedded ward. The words, printed so small and contained in a table became distorted. Oh my god I think I might be about to cry. I panicked. I didn't recognise the words or acronyms for the medical conditions and diagnoses. The letters that formed obscure looking aboriginal names, poked at my eyes like acupuncture needles as I held tightly onto the handover sheet with my shaking hands. My brain was numb with apprehension and anxiety until terror took over as the Clinical Nurse Manager looked at me and introduced me to the staff. All eyes were on me and I felt the urge to run away.

Had I made a huge mistake, had it been too long since I last worked in an acute area? Well, I was about to find out. The handover turned into a babbling haze as the staff from the morning shift took turns to come in and update us on the patients from the list that they had cared for that morning. When all the patients had been discussed, the staff allocation was announced. I was buddied up with another UK nurse called Leanne, and I felt relief as we left the confines of the handover room. The relief was shortlived. We collected and signed for our keys to the drugs room and our pagers, which had to be worn and responded to at all times, and were just about to start introducing ourselves to our allocated patients for the afternoon when the emergency code blue alarm rang through our pagers and over the public address system.

"Stand back!" Leanne shouted and put her arm out in front of my chest.

'Good call,' I thought, a few moments later, when as I stepped back against the wall, the resuscitation team hurtled down the corridor toward me.

The red-and-white resuscitation trolley, being driven by the medical ward team leader Fiona, led the team. In her wake were the intensive care team, the nurse coordinator, junior doctors and a consultant. They were rushing to one of our patients. When the team had all arrived at room 14, we approached from behind to be the backup, in case any other equipment or medicines were required. The controlled melee that ensued is a memory that I will never forget. After only ten minutes the patient was stabilised; and complete with bed, portable monitors and intravenous fluids, he was being transferred to the intensive care unit. This well-choreographed piece of work, that I witnessed and would be involved in many times over the coming years, had saved the life of a young aboriginal man. After starting the shift in a blaze of adrenaline the remainder was calm and controlled. By the time the night shift arrived to take over I had found my rhythm and was looking forward to coming back in the morning to do it all again.

I had not lost my confidence after all; I loved it, I was a nurse and I could still do it. It was just like recovering after a fall from your bike, the cure is to get back on and pedal as fast as you can. The graduate nurse program, which is very successful in Alice Springs, was a motivating experience. Newly qualified nurses who are eager to gain practical skills experience were stimulating for nurses similar to me, who have been qualified for many years, to always be up to date and able to provide support.

I was also very fortunate to be given the opportunity to open and manage the new twenty-bedded Continuing Care Ward (CCW) in February 2009. The unit was opened to accommodate the increasing need for high quality care and support during the rehabilitation and transitional care stages of recovery from trauma and complications of chronic disease. The introduction of individualised care packages, concentrating on maximising their physical potential, aimed to facilitate an increased rate of successful discharges back into their communities and homes.

Working in the role of Clinical Nurse Manager on the continuing care ward was one of the most rewarding nursing experiences I have ever had. Our philosophy, especially in relation to ensuring and achieving patient-centred care, focused on an allied health care team approach. With the staff of all grades participating in a variety of aspects of holistic care provision, the sense of achievement felt by helping people return to their communities with the ability to cope with permanent disabilities after a stroke or motor vehicle accident, etc. was very rewarding. Far from being demoralised, the team on the continuing care ward provided a valuable service and I feel very privileged to have worked with a great team of discharge planners, educators, clinical nurses, patient care assistants, physiotherapists, occupational therapists, resident doctors and consultants. I think it is also important to acknowledge the enormous role and impact that the volunteer service had on our ward, and in the hospital as a whole.

The Drover volunteers are a well-organised group, who provide a valuable support service in Alice Springs Hospital. Apart from the huge amount of fundraising they do, for equipment and services, they also contribute their time to assist the hospital staff. Drover volunteers provide tea and coffee rounds in the Emergency Department. They operate the hospital information desk, complete ward visits to offer books and pastimes for patients on the wards, as well as helping out with transport for patients outside the hospital with their team of drivers.

It is often a hard task to intervene with essential services without compromising cultural beliefs. 'Sorry business', which is the aboriginal practice of mourning the death or separation from an aboriginal family member, was probably one of the most alarming spectacles that I witnessed as a culturally naive English nurse arriving in Alice Springs. The first death on the medical ward occurred just a week after my arrival. It was announced with chanting, followed loud wailing from the aboriginal women in attendance. Some of them started stripping off their clothes, almost ripping at them, but despite this, the moaning and weeping continued. As they started walking around the ward performing this audible out-pouring of grief, I have to admit to being somewhat frightened. The commotion acted like an incentive for more people to arrive and participate.

When the aboriginal men started gathering, an aura of tension developed. The hospital security guards and the Aboriginal Liaison Officers attended, to ensure that the grieving family and friends remained in one area. I had witnessed this gathering and clan-like grouping in the town, outside bars and bottle-shops, and I prayed beneath my breath that no one would remove their shirt, as this was a sign that a fight or attack was imminent. The policy on allowing culturally acceptable grieving was carefully implemented and in doing this the risk of the tension igniting into anything more sinister was abated.

Alice Springs Hospital utilises a service consisting of Aboriginal Liaison Officers who support, interpret and advise on the cultural acceptability of procedures and importantly how to integrate disabled people back into their communities with care and attention to acceptable interventions. Aboriginal culture is a fascinating and huge subject which I am not qualified to write about, but I learnt a great deal from my outback experience, which I have carried with me since then.

The underlying problems are largely around aspects of Western culture being introduced, principally alcohol supply and consumption, which has led to dependency issues, domestic violence, thefts and crime to support dependency habits. You may say that all societies have these issues and you would be right. However, it is intensified when added to a large transient, multi-cultural population confined in a small town in the desert; think of a soda bottle being shaken with no one wanting to take the lid off. The emergency services such as the Royal Flying Doctors Services (RFDS) play a significant role in facilitating access to healthcare across the Northern Territory, especially for the outlying communities. Nursing staff are offered the opportunity to go out for the day with the RFDS and experience first-hand the challenges they face while collecting, treating and transporting patients from the outback and indigenous communities. The aim is to help give a greater understanding of the physical condition in which some patients are received at the hospital.

As a Registered General Nurse at Alice Springs Hospital, some basic things are different and challenging from the outset. Firstly, there is a language barrier. Although the majority of patients speak and understand some English, some indigenous people do not know or understand any English. Therefore, the interpreter services are crucial, especially in an emergency, to ensure the patient and their family understand what is happening. Secondly, there are culturally unacceptable issues like direct eye contact and male / female chaperoning contact to consider. Thirdly, on a more basic level, there are simple differences between UK and Australian healthcare procedures. Therefore, despite your level of skill and experience, everyone starts as a novice until you understand the basics.

As the workforce includes staff from all around the world, you find yourself working with staff from Asia, India and the Philippines, which also have some language implications. Although everyone achieving employment on a visa has to meet an approved level of English language skills, the family member of nurses who may undertake ancillary posts can have a more limited English language comprehension, therefore the reality is that understanding each other still presents issues and challenges. Whereas Australians have inflections and tones and some tend to use a lot of slang and informal phrases, people from the UK tend to speak faster than Australians. Depending on where in the UK they are from, if you add in the regional dialects of people from Liverpool, Glasgow or Manchester, for example, then sometimes there is scope for misunderstandings. Other accents and terminology differences also keep you on your guard when you first arrive. Having said this, you very quickly learn to adopt some Australian and Aboriginal words and phrases without which some patients have no idea as to what you are referring. For example, G'day = (Hello); tucker = (food); pica = (pain); snags = (sausages); grog = (alcohol.)

The most noticeable differences are that the aboriginal people tend to leave it longer before they seek medical attention, almost leaving it too late in some cases. This results in a higher demand for intensive and critical care beds. The knock on effect of this is that more intensive interventions are required, such as the immediate use of intravenous antibiotics instead of the opportunity to use oral treatments, thus increasing the risk of complications. Secondly, the amount and severity of traumatic, alcohol-induced injuries is far more that you would see in a UK hospital emergency department. The use of almost primitive weapons like axes, sticks and household items is shocking initially: the sad thing for me is that you very quickly accept it as the norm. I berated myself many times during my time at ASH when I felt I was accepting the normality of witnessing physical abuse between family members, which is never acceptable in any culture. Motor vehicles accidents (MVA) are another major problem. Many indigenous people from the outlying town camps drive vehicles that appear, and often are, not road-worthy. This combined with alcohol consumption and sometimes no formal driving test or experience is a recipe for disaster.

The percentage of people suffering from some form of chronic disease is an additional burden to healthcare services. The indigenous population have some of the highest levels of diabetes type 2 and heart disease principally due to poor diet and lifestyle choices. One thing you notice on arrival in Alice Springs is the amount and popularity of fast food, especially deep fried chicken. Even within the hospital environment, it is sad to see patients walk, or be taken in a wheelchair, to the canteen for their deep fried chicken. Others have it brought in from Kentucky Fried Chicken by friends and family. Despite multiple health campaigns and outreach clinics for preventative medicine the culture of unhealthy eating of cheap, fast food affects all ages. The co-morbidities of high blood pressure, high cholesterol and obesity increase the demand for healthcare services for both in-and-out-patients.

A zero tolerance for alcohol in the hospital leads to patients Taking their Own Leave (TOL) and going to the local bars, or watering holes as they are often referred to in Australia. The nearest to the hospital and the most popular amongst indigenous patients was the Gap View Hotel. It is a regular sight to see the daytime security staff, which included Nigel who regularly worked there, refusing entry to people wearing hospital identity bracelets, hospital issue green pyjamas and sometimes patients holding medical equipment like IV pumps and catheter bags.

The other form of disease which places a high demand on health care services is renal disease. The amount of indigenous people requiring renal dialysis is another sad statistic in Alice Springs, due to kidney disease and trauma. The high incidence of physical disability from trauma and amputations resulting from diabetes dictates the need for the hospital to have its own wheelchair and prosthetic clinics and workshops. They aim to provide patients with some degree of mobility and independence within their community. Wheelchairs are a valued possession and often finding one to move patients between departments in the hospital can be difficult as they 'disappear' frequently and despite highly visible signs attached to them it is not unusual to see them at Coles or Woolworth's supermarkets, or abandoned outside hotels or bars.

Alice Springs is known as a 'marmite' town to us pommes, meaning you either love it or hate it. Nursing here offers wide-ranging opportunities for promotion and for some it has the ability to become a permanent home with a great lifestyle, if you can accept the challenges and compromises in exchange for the benefits on offer. It is, in my opinion, definitely an experience worth having at least once.

Chapter 5
Happy times in the desert

While writing this book, I tried to capture the essence of our triumph over adversity using the power of positive thoughts and actions. In doing so, I discovered the bad times easily monopolising my thoughts, which I felt could give a negative perspective to my story. Is this because they are still quite raw to think or talk about? It seems to take more effort, memory and recall to recount the good and happy times, especially when you have been overwhelmed by grief and despair. It is important however to remember that we went to Australia to 'live the dream' and, for the majority of our time there, we did just that.

We achieved many of the goals we set out to, and some we had not anticipated. We enjoyed some memorable family occasions and embraced living the dream that we left the UK to pursue. This chapter focuses on a few of the memorable occasions and experiences we had during our time in Alice Springs. I think it helps to give a sense of balance for what was to come, adding some perspective. I also hope it will help to make sense of some of the decisions we went on to make as our adventure developed.

Alice Springs and the Northern Territory have some amazing cultural and environmental attractions; we were privileged to experience a few of these during our time in Australia.

Kings Canyon – Northern Territory

In July 2008, Nigel and I took our first Australian romantic weekend break. Just the two of us, as Jaime stayed with Teresa, Paul and the girls in Alice Springs. We drove to the Kings Canyon resort in the Watarrka National Park. It is between 315 and 475 kilometres from Alice Springs, depending on whether you take the four-wheel drive route or the bitumen road route. We completed both, taking one route there and the other on the return trip. The scenery and wildlife, especially on the four-wheel drive route, were spectacular. Despite July being wintertime there is no respite from the extreme temperatures. Therefore, it was not only refreshing, but also breath-taking to unwind from the car journey in our personal Jacuzzi bath in our hotel room. The unfrosted bathroom windows overlooked rocky hills and scrubland frequented only by the resident wildlife of wallabies, etc.

The word 'paradise' can conjure up visions of tropical islands, white sandy beaches, clear blue oceans and ultimate relaxation. However, in the desert paradise comes in the contrasting form of idyllic seclusion, at one with some of nature's wildest inhabitants i.e. dingoes, wallabies and snakes, in luxurious surroundings. We undertook the six-kilometre Kings Canyon Rim Walk which starts with the five hundred steps up to the rim with astonishingly breath-taking views when you reach the top lookout onto and into the canyon.

Sarah Jane at top of Kings Canyon

At the top of the canyon, the cliffs are more than three hundred metres high and they descend down to the 'Garden Of Eden' and 'Kings Creek' at the bottom. The canyon has attracted and enthralled people for millions of years, and some parts of the gorge are located in sacred Aboriginal sites and protected by law. We had some amazing moments and experiences on this romantic break and the memories will stay with me forever.

Mother and daughter reunited

I hugged Samantha so tight, saying goodbye on a squally winter's night in January 2008, and cried the whole of the five-hour coach trip to Heathrow airport. The unrelenting tears were my tribute to our love. On our arrival in Alice Springs, I was unpacking and found a CD in my suitcase. It was a homemade compilation by Samantha entitled, 'Don't forget me': of course I started to cry again. The songs were from films that Samantha and I had enjoyed watching together over the years, 'Mamma Mia;' 'Four weddings and a Funeral,' etc. There were also songs with lyrics that portrayed some of the feelings we had drifted through in the months prior to our departure.

Samantha and I have always been close. When I was first divorced, as a single mum living with only Samantha and Robert for a few years, we did everything together. Those years formed bonds that cannot be broken. Therefore, the prospect of her celebrating her 21st birthday in the UK away from me was out of the question. Samantha, and her partner Doug, arrived in Alice Springs at the end of November 2008. They would be staying for two-and-half weeks, which would include her 21st birthday on the 7th December 2008, when she also became engaged.

Nigel, Sarah Jane, Samantha and Jaime:
Anzac Hill, Alice Springs – December 2008

I had booked annual leave from work and Nigel had a few days off for some of the trips we had arranged. This included taking them to one of our favourite places, Kings Canyon and arranging for a bottle of champagne to be placed in their suite on arrival.

With Samantha in the house, her familiar continuous chatter

resounding all day, everything felt wonderful. For me as her mum who had missed her so badly, I now was complete again. We spent time together relaxing in the pool, sitting outside late into the evening with a glass of wine; it felt like old times and as if we had never been apart. I knew that I had missed her since our departure, but I had totally under-estimated how much until we were together again. During their stay, Samantha and Doug experienced hot-air ballooning at dawn, a helicopter ride, camel riding and so much more. It was amazing having barbecues at the Old Telegraph Station, picnics, shopping and showing her our new life in Australia. As usual, the goodbyes were the hardest, but worth it for the time we spent together.

Our new additions: Dave and Buster

One of the most joyful events in Alice Springs was when we acquired our two 'boys', Dave and Buster. They are Australian cattle dogs, which are a mix of kelpie and blue heeler breeds. We bought Dave from my friend Sue, a nurse on the medical ward, whose dog had an unplanned litter of puppies. Although we were looking for a guard dog, Dave caught my eye. However, he was the smallest, runty looking specimen you would ever see, with black and white markings not dissimilar to a cow.

"Not much potential as a guard dog there," Nigel said as I picked Dave up from the blanket on the floor. I knew Dave was the one, regardless of his guarding potential.

With Dave settled in at home, I have to be honest, I did not adhere to the rules Nigel set for rearing a guard dog, especially when he was at work. Dave was supposed to sleep on the porch of the outdoor entertainment area. This would enable him to run around the garden and patrol the fences, barking to alert us to intruders. However, with Nigel working long night shifts I would sit outside with Dave, until about ten or eleven o'clock in the evening. Then he would look at me with his sad eyes and I would take him in with me. I felt sorry for him outside alone and he was a good boy indoors. I always had him back outside before Nigel came home, so our secret was safe, until now:

sorry Nigel. We sat and cuddled most evenings and he was like a replacement child for the ones left behind. We shared my Weetabix in the mornings, and he loved lying on the sun-lounger with me when I got home from work in the afternoon. We would watch Jaime have her after-school swim or play on the trampoline, as Nigel slept ready for the night shift.

It soon became apparent that for the hours that I was at work and Jaime was at school Dave needed some company. We decided that we would get him a friend. Instead of looking for another puppy, we thought we would get a dog from the RSPCA rescue centre and went one afternoon for a look around. In my mind, Dave would remain in charge as the guard dog, of sorts, so I was looking for a small scruffy lap dog needing a good home. However, as we entered the kennel area at the RSPCA rescue centre, a dog that looked familiar in its mannerisms and stance pushed his head up against the wire netting door.

Nigel and I looked at him and both said, "He looks like Dave."

We enquired about the nervous bundle of merle and white that cowered when anyone went near. His name was Buster, and he had been taken to the rescue centre because his owner could not cope with him in their small courtyard garden. He was not getting the attention, or exercise, he required and it was obvious that he had not had a good start in life.

Dave and Buster 2009

We decided immediately that he was to be our new addition,

subject to us being assessed as a suitable adoptive family for him of course. Therefore, to start the process we had to take Dave to visit Buster in the exercise yard, so that they could see if they would get on together. Nigel completed the introductory visits with Dave to the RSPCA centre. He described after his visits how, initially and quite normally being wary of each other, they later demonstrated a sense of togetherness and played in synchronisation. This seemed strange, but reassuringly was lovely to watch. We eventually brought our second dog home and got off to a shaky start when the territorial stand-offs took place as Buster, our new addition, entered Dave's yard. It was during this heated scuffle that Nigel decided to try to intervene and break them up. He got a deep, penetrating bite wound on his forearm for his efforts – lesson learnt, do not try to break up fighting dogs.

'Our boys', as we refer to them now, settled in well together; later we were to establish that Buster's previous owner had been a healthcare assistant at the hospital, and that she had bought one of Sue's puppies at the same time as I bought Dave. In a twist of fate, Dave and Buster were now reunited, brothers together again. The 'boys' bring us so much pleasure, and accompanied us on many adventures, both as a family and with Nigel alone, as you will discover later. They totally care and look out for one another and ironically, they have become the best guard dogs ever, despite my interventions.

Camping and leisure pursuits Alice Springs style

Nigel, Jaime and I had many family adventures in the desert of the Northern Territory, most of which involved camping in riverbeds at Owen Springs Reserve or Red Bank Gorge. Getting used to camping in the wild with dingoes, snakes, spiders and kangaroos surrounding you was very different from camping in the peak district or in Cornwall. It would soon become 'normal' to see a camel walking at the side of the road as we drove off on a Friday afternoon for a weekend camping in the riverbed.

The wildlife in the desert did not interfere with our fun, although the constant awareness for personal safety, especially for Jaime, in

relation to spiders in the tent and sleeping bag, took some
reinforcement. However, I never got used to having dingoes around
me. On one particular weekend we were camping at Owen Springs; it
was after midnight, but there was a full moon and the moonlight
permeated through the fly netting roof of our swag.

A swag, sometimes called a bedroll, is a waterproof canvas sleeping
capsule which has fly netting to also make it insect-proof when you
peel back the canvas layer. Swags have a foam mattress, on which you
lay your sleeping bag. When rolled up they are lightweight and
compact, making it easy to transport on camping adventures. Swags
are still in use in the outback by drovers (roaming ranch hands). We
had a double swag, which was cosy, and I loved that you could lay and
watch the moon and the stars in bed, which is very romantic, and you
really appreciate the lack of light pollution when you camp in the
desert. As temperatures at night in the desert can fall to zero they are
also very snug and warm with your sleeping bag inside, so perfect for
daytime escape from the midday sun and warmth at night. We have
even put our swag up beside the car at the side of the road when
driving interstate. Anyway, I digress.

As usual when camping, Dave was in his wire cage positioned
outside our swag. It was normal for Dave to do a single 'woof' if a
snake slithered by during the night and that usually sufficed to keep
the campsite clear of slithering intruders. However, on this occasion
once Dave started barking he did not stop. Nigel, realising something
or someone must be in our camp area, grabbed the torch, opened the
swag and quietly opened the cage to put Dave's lead on. Immediately
the torchlight went on Dave, who was still barking, lurched forward
taking Nigel with him. In front of them was a pack of dingoes. In
hindsight, Nigel now admits, what happened next was impulsive and
ill thought through. Nigel and Dave set off after the pack of dingoes,
which had turned to exit the camp area. This could have gone horribly
wrong if they had turned and tried to stand their ground, as they could
have attacked both Nigel and Dave. Undeterred, Nigel and Dave broke
out into a full-on run behind the pack of dingoes, and soon they were
well away from camp. When Nigel and Dave returned, they both went

back to sleep as if nothing had happened. I, however, was recalling dingo horror stories of stealing babies from tents and ransacking ill-prepared tourists in the desert.

Camping in the river bed

Outback camping was a wonderful experience for Jaime. It gave her the freedom to experience outdoors pursuits within the various places in which we camped. She climbed gum trees, made secret camps in fallen eucalyptus trees, rolled in sand dunes as she explored everything her new Australian life had to offer. She even helped to dig the dunny, the Australian slang word for a toilet. Sometimes we would let her bring a friend on our camping trips and they would enjoy cooking marshmallows on the campfire, collecting firewood playing Frisbee etc. The girls' tent was always out of bounds to 'the parents' in the evening when giggling, eating sweets and story-telling went on, not of ghosts and vampires, but of outback adventures.

The availability of leisure facilities in Alice Springs enables access to animals and activities for all ages. Jaime, who loved sports and outdoor games, revelled in our family picnics and barbeques at the Old Telegraph Station on a Sunday or a visit to the Traeger Park sports arena or town swimming pool. For a more leisurely trip out, Jaime and I would visit the Olive Pink Botanical Gardens tea-rooms with Carol after school, or on the weekend we would go the Alice Springs Desert Park or Reptile Centre with Teresa, Abigail and Lauren. We attended the ballet at The Araluen Centre for Arts and Entertainment, and Jaime even performed in the Eisteddfod there as a choir member for

Lutheran Living Waters school choir.

There are so many amazing places to experience in and around Alice Springs, which is one reason why it is a tourist hot spot with many tour companies operating day and overnight tours to the sights and spectacles that are unique to the area. I particularly loved being able to swim in open water holes at Ormiston Gorge, whereas Nigel took on personal challenges like rock climbing and amateur boxing.

Events unique to Alice Springs include firstly, the Finke Desert Race, which is an annual event held on the Queen's Birthday long weekend. It is a gruelling off-road race that runs from Alice Springs to the Finke community, then back again the following day. The total length of the race is roughly five hundred kilometres. It attracts spectators from around the world, some of whom camp along the length of the track. Each year approximately five hundred competitors on buggies and motorbikes make this the biggest sporting event in the Alice Springs sporting calendar. Secondly, a unique sporting event for a desert location is the Henley-on-Todd Regatta, also known as the Todd River Race. This race is held annually in the dry Todd River bed. It is a sand river race with bottomless boats, manned by contestants in fancy dress, and it is the only dry river regatta in the world. Thirdly, another unusual sporting event is the Camel Cup, an annual event that takes place at the local racecourse in Alice Springs. It is a full day of racing with camels, instead of horses, but also incorporating other events such as the 'fashions on the field contest', which are more commonly associated with horseracing.

The positive focus of family-centred activities, created at the community events in Australia, is something I never experienced in the UK in all my years as a parent there. Jaime has had some amazing experiences and opportunities in the Northern Territory, Queensland and Tasmania and has made some great friends.

Chapter 6
Long distance parenting

From the moment we decided to move to Australia, we were acutely aware of the implications of long-distance parenting. When the permission for Jaime to leave the UK was finally in our hands, the harsh reality of leaving the other children really hit home. With only a matter of days between obtaining permission to leave the UK and the granting of our visa, the flights were booked; and all the scenarios, plans for communicating and visits, that we had all discussed, suddenly seemed very inadequate for what was to be the biggest move of all of our lives.

Robert, my eldest son from my first marriage, travelled with us to Alice Springs, when we left the UK in January 2008. However, he was too far away from his greatest love - surfing. Robert loves the sea and surfing; and has done since his early teens. It was no surprise when he made plans to travel and experience the Australian surfing Meccas. Robert travelled from Alice Springs to Queensland initially, visiting amongst other places, Brisbane, Proserpine, and The Whitsundays, before finally travelling onto Manly Beach, in Sydney. Knowing, he was still in Australia, made being there for him as a parent much easier, especially as he was eighteen, and most of the support a teenage boy needs at that age when travelling is financial! Robert eventually returned to the UK later that year to start a new job, and coincidentally, a new relationship.

As part of our visit and communication plan, devised before we left, we had built into our good intentions the fact that I would not be able to take annual leave for six months, due to my work contract. Nigel would therefore need to return to the UK alone on this first visit, to see Clair, Phillip and Samantha, (and as it turned out, Robert, who was then back in the UK,) in August 2008. Arranging this first visit back to the UK for Nigel was relatively easy, logistically. He would pick up a hire car at Heathrow airport, and be a free agent, to squeeze in as much time as the children's school summer holidays, and the older children's work commitments, would allow. It was terribly hard to stay in Alice Springs while Nigel was away with the other children. Even though photographs and updates frequently appeared on Facebook, to show Jaime and me, where they were going and what they were doing, it was not the same as being there. I missed them so much. This was to be the first sign of how our lives, and those of our children, had changed because of our international move. Would we ever get used to being away from the children? I did not miss the UK, but as we would find out over the coming two years, not being there physically when the children needed us, especially on a psychological level, would become harder to cope with as time went on.

The new family buzzwords, Skype and social media, principally Facebook. Before we left the UK, we all had Facebook profiles set up and Robert, our IT whiz had even been patient enough to teach me how to use Skype. We ensured that everyone had the tools and resources for regular Facebook and Skype chats to take place. In the planning, this was easy, achievable and sounded ideal, as they say in Cornwall. However, the time differences, shift work, school and time constraints would challenge everyone's commitment. All of our powers of patience and tolerance would be tested over the coming years.

Some difficulties were harder to deal with than others: for example, after Samantha became engaged on her twenty-first birthday in Alice Springs 2008, her wedding date was set for 11th January 2011. I never realised how remote from the arrangements I would feel. Despite regular emails with samples, prices, links to venues, wedding dresses, cakes, etc. it was not the same as being there, and planning it all with her. In reality, whether or not I would have been more involved had I still been living in the UK is hard to say. However, I still feel we both missed out on certain elements of the wedding preparation experience. In hindsight, I also question if I would or could have spotted the warning signs that her intended marriage would not last.

Dealing with crisis from afar.

When the children celebrated happy, memorable times after we left, it was our disappointment at not being there to share it with them which dominated our thoughts. One particular example was graduation and prom night for Clair and Molly; again in reality whether or not we would have been able to be involved is debatable, given our ex-partners were involved, but having to look at the photographs on Facebook of the preparation, the dresses, the staged family pictures was extremely hard. Missing birthdays, anniversaries and graduations was difficult enough; however, when times were tough for the children it was challenging as well as frustrating. When they had some form of personal crisis to deal with, it became increasingly difficult to rationalise our decision to be so far away.

There are times when all you want, or need to do is to give them a hug, and be there to listen to them, even if on a practical level you cannot help. In March 2011, when Samantha endured the breakdown of her marriage, within the first three months, I could easily have returned to support her. However, as luck would have it, she decided to come home to the family that loved and missed her in Australia, to let us help her through this traumatic, personal experience.

Coping with the issues, good and bad, of long distance parenting, has also added positive aspects to the relationships that we now have with the children. Everybody made more effort to write letters, post presents, email photographs or post them on Facebook etc., to make sure we were all up to speed with everyone's life events. When we lived closer to the children in the UK, the majority of the communicating with the children as they progressed through the teenage years, was about curfews, transport to friends' houses for parties, pocket money and day-to-day things. We did not really have long discussions on a regular basis, about their lives, their friends; and to be honest they had little interest in our lives, we were just 'the parents.' This new, in-depth aspect to our relationships was a big addition while we were in Australia, and it has given them all a greater sense of responsibility for maintaining relationships.

There have been many times, throughout our journey, although principally in Queensland, when our physical location, i.e. living in the 'woods,' or after the floods, made maintaining our contact with the children difficult, both technically and financially. For example, when we were living in the 'woods,' in Millmerran, we managed with mobile phones, offering value-added packages for international calls and an internet dongle, which plugs into the laptop on a 'pay as you go' tariff. We did all of this, and more, to keep regular, quality contact with our children. Even when the rains came, we would not be cut off from the children. When mobile network reception was poor, or non-existent, we used the internet at the local libraries, or cafes, proving that 'where there's a will, there's a way.'

The important lesson learnt was, that a relationship, whether it is a friend or family member, takes effort on both parts. A relationship which operates with only one person making an effort always leaves the other person feeling disappointed and neglected. We ensured from day one, that communication was the key ingredient to the success of our new life in Australia, without jeopardising our relationships with the children.

Throughout all the trials and tribulations, both in the UK and in Australia, over the last four-and-a-half years, we have been there for the children, in whatever form we could, and importantly, they have been there for us. The pivotal element is the 'importance of family,' and this should never be under-estimated or take for granted. I sometimes wonder if my perceived 'gaps' in my life, relating to the absence of my father, and losing custody of Molly, make me fight harder, to hold our family together. By utilising a set of good, positive values, I think overall, as a family, we have been successful. Of course, only time will tell.

As a child, you cannot really understand or appreciate the responsibility, guilt and variety of feelings that a parent experiences while trying to provide the best life they can for their child, until that is the day comes when you become a parent. From that day forward, you are responsible for your child, their every need, not only physical, but also emotional, spiritual and psychological. Parenting is a wonderful experience, and even though there are times when you feel like there is no time in your life for anything that is 'just about you,' the rewards come, when you see your grown up children achieving their goals: happy, healthy and appreciative for all that life has to offer them. I am proud to be a mum, and a step-mum.

Chapter 7
Educating Jaime in Alice Springs

When you have school-age children, any change that involves a transfer to a new school, requires detailed identification of the educational opportunities in the new location. When you add into this equation a child with dyslexia and an international move to an Australian outback town, the pressure on the research intensifies. Informed decision-making to ensure that the best possible educational resources are available, and that overseas pupils can easily access them, is vital to the success of the move. The Alice Springs area has nineteen public and private schools. They cater for local and remote area students and therefore you would think that choice was not going to be an issue for us. Our success in the primary school setting led us into a false sense of security, as our new life unfolded.

The timing of our move needed to coincide with the start of the new school year, which in Australia is late January in comparison to September in the UK. Even though we could have moved at any point, we wanted to make this process as easy as possible for Jaime, and starting mid-year can be traumatic and disruptive for any child. Starting with other new children takes away the isolation, and feeling that everyone's attention is only on you, that can happen in this situation. There had been more than enough isolation and attention focused on Jaime in this process already. With this in mind, and due to the requirements of the court proceedings to obtain our permission to emigrate, the pressure was on us to make the right choices, and to demonstrate our rationale. We have successfully educated all the older children, so why did we now feel like complete novices to the parenting and educational system? The answer was the pressure to get it right. There would be no second chances.

One of our reasons for choosing to apply for a work-sponsored visa in Alice Springs was that Nigel already had family there. We knew that Jaime would need extended family support, especially in her new school environment, after leaving her friends and siblings behind. Jaime had been with us when we visited Nigel's cousin Teresa, her husband Paul and their children Abigail and Lauren during our holiday to Australia in 2007. With this relationship, which had been nurtured by Skype, letters and regular contact during the visa process in place, together with their professional and local knowledge, we were confident that this would help us make well-informed choices for Jaime's education.

Paul is a teacher at the Yirara College, which is part of the Lutheran Church. Yirara, located on the outskirts of Alice Springs, is a boarding college catering for teenage indigenous students from the remote communities. Teresa is a teacher's aide at the Living Waters Lutheran primary school, and together they were able to provide us with in-depth knowledge, not only from their personal and professional experience but also from their friends who had experienced a move to Alice Springs from interstate or overseas. We felt very fortunate to have access to these personal resources and testimonials as we researched our options, especially in relation to Jaime's special educational needs, as this was a key element that had to be right. Making the decision to enrol Jaime at the Living Waters School, knowing that Teresa, Abigail and Lauren would all be there, albeit in different classes, was reassuring. It felt like the pieces of this part of our emigration puzzle were starting to fit together perfectly.

The ability to be able to afford private schooling for Jaime was a first for any of our children. Having always had at least three or four of our children living with us at any one time, and given the lack of financial support for working class people to access private education in the UK, all of our children had been educated in the public system. Nonetheless, they have all done extremely well, going on to college, university and good jobs. For Jaime, assessed as dyslexic and dysnumeric just a year before we emigrated, being able to give her this unique opportunity to access a higher standard of support for her educational needs was a huge bonus. With both of us working, on salaries far in excess of anything we had earned in the UK, this was an ideal opportunity to invest in her future. From the day of her first dyslexia assessment, we strived to prevent her from being labelled as if she had some form of disease or affliction. We knew how cruel her peers could and would be, and how hard school life is without any additional issues. That said, to get the help she needs, it always has to be talked about and added to school files and reports and I dislike that with a passion. The negative atmosphere that surrounds us whenever we have to say it or write it, infers that Jaime is needy or different. No one wants to feel different for perceived negative reasons. We all strive to be special or different in positive ways, for our skills, accomplishments or achievements. Therefore, I knew that one day Jaime would despise this labelling process, and I was right. I wanted it to be different for her in Australia, naïve probably, hopeful always.

We decided to give Jaime's education a further head start, also enabling her to make friends prior to progressing to high school the following year. With her birthday being in September, we were able to take advantage of a window of opportunity for her to repeat the final year of primary school in Australia. This extra time would enable her to have access to one-to-one support for her dyslexia, and be able to continue the toe-by-toe program she had commenced in the UK.

On arrival, the first noticeable difference was the class sizes. These were noticeably smaller than her previous school, at around twenty children per class as a maximum, compared to the UK average of thirty. Jaime had no problems integrating into her new class or school. She started Japanese classes, joined the school choir and took part in many after-school physical activities and clubs. These new opportunities were possible due to the Australian climate and the heightened focus on health and exercise in young children, the aim of which was to promote and assist in the prevention of chronic disease, which is rife in Alice Springs. The sense of relief we felt as Jaime adapted so easily to schooling in Australia was immense. We knew that this one decision, amongst the many we had made during the process, had been a significant issue and was pivotal to the court proceedings being a success. In addition, having put all of our faith in the Australian education system to back up our decision-making, we could now see first-hand that Jaime was happy and making friends, giving us the final confirmation that we had made the right decision, especially as far as her education was concerned, which was perfect.

Repeating the final year of primary schooling had been a great opportunity and advantage for Jaime and when the time came for the move up to high school, her reading age had improved as had her numeracy skills. The toe-by-toe program had taught her skills that boosted her literacy confidence and, together with the friends she had made, we had no concerns about the next stage in her education. Jaime's graduation ceremony from Living Waters Primary school happened to coincide with Samantha's visit to Australia, and so she attended with me. I felt so proud, and still do, that against the odds, Jaime is a fighter like her mum.

Jaime started St Phillips College, Alice Springs, in January 2009 and although she started with other children from Living Waters primary school, the transition was not entirely smooth. Even though there were more support networks and opportunities available to Jaime, it was obvious very quickly that she was struggling in this environment. The school and its staff were convinced that Jaime's educational difficulties were the root cause. They arranged for hearing tests, eyesight assessments and most invasively of all, psychological assessment and counselling for Jaime and us as a family. The reminders of the CAFCASS scenario loomed as Nigel, Jaime and I had to answer questions about the move and the distance from family as a possible contributing factor.

Feelings of guilt and inadequacy haunted me as Jaime's dyslexia struck again at her confidence. I knew the move to Australia had been the best opportunity and experience for Jaime as she was so happy and fulfilled outside of school. She had so many friends, interests and talents, so why did this new school environment have such a negative and profound effect on her?

It was disappointing when eventually we discovered, after months of scrutiny, that the main reason for her unhappiness at school was not about us as parents or us as a family but was the result of bullying by American schoolchildren in relation to her dyslexia. This prestigious private school, which caters for some very intelligent children aged between twelve and eighteen, demonstrated a noticeable intolerance of students who were less able. The less able were deemed to 'get in the way' of their progress, or were 'stupid' in comparison to their perceived greater abilities. Jaime is not stupid by any means, but as in many life experiences, if someone tells you enough times that you are inadequate or stupid in the end the risk is that it will be believed.

After weeks of help, assistance and assessment, in collaboration with the school chaplain and the St Phillips head master, we decided it was time for change. With no improvement at school and Jaime now the unhappiest we had seen her since our arrival in Australia, there was no choice but to enrol her into another school. As a family, we were determined not to let this episode affect Jaime in a negative way. Even after accessing all the resources provided by the teaching staff and the chaplain it was not an easy decision to make to remove her from St Phillips. However, we could not risk tarnishing her newfound educational confidence with juvenile harassment.

Assuring Jaime that something positive would come from this experience, even though at the time we struggled to see what that could be, my mission was to find a solution. After many school visits and researching of curriculums and special needs support services, we decided to put Jaime into the Northern Territory State school system, enrolling her at the Centralian Middle school. With diminished confidence, we felt completely unsure about whether the state school system could support Jaime, or if she would be able to integrate into a school with a high proportion of indigenous students. My heart was heavy at the prospect, but I had to believe that this was the answer and that she would be happy in school again. Therefore, imagine our delight and surprise when the staff gave her more support and had more resources available for her due to the significant government funding they received.

Jaime flourished in her new school, and as a direct result she became more confident and more involved with learning practical skills for life after school. When we asked her what had made the difference, she said that she felt the pressure of being 'perfect in her written work and maths had been lifted', and even though it was still an integral part of her school day, the teaching methods obviously made it less stressful and more achievable for her.

Chapter 8
It's Christmas, but not as we know it.

What have we done?

Our first Christmas in Australia was always going to be a tough and testing time for us. However, we naïvely thought we had prepared for it, by reappraising ourselves of the benefits of our new location and lifestyle. December is summer time in Australia, with guaranteed good weather, and plenty to do and be involved in. However, there were few signs of the festive season in our house and my heart was heavy. I felt utterly miserable and empty inside. In theory, we were 'living the dream,' so what was wrong with me? Would any of the new improvements, to our lifestyle, really numb the pain that I was feeling? Despite delving into my hitherto bottomless reserve of positivity, the simple answer was 'no'.

The heartache I already felt, due to the physical separation from the older children worsened as Christmas approached. The almost hourly emotional rollercoaster journeyed, peaking then sinking, as the mere thought of it being just the three of us loomed ever closer. Christmas would be poles apart from anything we were familiar with in the UK. In the past it was always about us as a family: a big, complicated, but loving family. As a blended or stepfamily, it always involved a great deal of commitment and logistical planning, in exchange for a lot of fun, happiness and laughter. Everyone, Jack excluded, strived to ensure that all of the children spent some of the Christmas and New Year period with each set of parents and stepparents, as well as extended family. This was not an easy feat to achieve; with the personalities involved, and having to contend with the tantrums of our ex partners when they did not get their own way. However, overall we achieved it; year after year, getting slightly better at it, as the children grew up and could verbalise their personal preferences. Obviously, there were times when not everyone always got the amount of time they would have hoped for or liked, but that goes with the walking on eggshells territory of divorce and child custody arrangements.

Here we were then, attempting Christmas in a new country. Alone, feeling deserted in the desert. In the height of the Australian summer, with daytime temperatures above forty-five degrees, it was in stark contrast to the UK December temperatures that we were familiar. In the UK, the temperatures at this time of year hover around zero, with everyone eager to see if there will be the elusive 'White Christmas.'

With our long-term dream firmly in our sights, albeit somewhat hazy at this moment in time, we decided that the best distraction was to embrace Australian culture. Socialising Australian style, and planning for the Australian tradition of the Christmas Day BBQ. This had to be the way forward. We were not feeling sociable, as you can imagine, but we needed to fit in with our work colleagues. However, we decided on a quiet affair, with just the three of us in the garden of our first home. It was a big milestone for us buying our first home together, something we could never have achieved in the UK. Our aim was to celebrate our first Christmas in Australia, and start making new memories. Our two outdoor entertaining areas, encased in shade cloth and bamboo, were enclosed in the generous rear garden. The swimming pool, a trampoline for Jaime and an area laid to lawn at the front, meant that we had all day access to sun, shade, activities and places to find sanctuary from the intense heat as the sun circled our domain.

I have to say, that in all honesty, in the run up to Christmas I was already feeling somewhat unsettled and deflated. Samantha and Doug had visited in early December to celebrate her 21st birthday with us, and when they returned home on the 10th, my feelings of separation anxiety were running high. It felt as if there was no festive spirit to be had, at least not as I remembered or wanted there to be. Despite going through the motions of the preparations with Jaime; such as putting up the Christmas tree, the lights, the array of homemade and purchased decorations, doing rounds of shopping, going to children's' parties and meals with friends, wrapping gifts, etc. I still was not feeling it at all. I am not sure if I should say Nigel was 'lucky enough' to experience a more outback Australian style Christmas at work, as there was little joy and goodwill to be had. It was mostly fights and police reports at the notorious 'Bojangles Saloon Bar', in the centre of Alice Springs. A popular hangout for backpackers, tourists and locals, he was working as a crowd controller, 'on the doors' or 'a bouncer' depending on the terminology you attach to it. It was peak season, therefore the number of tourists was high and many local families had seized the opportunity to holiday abroad or interstate to escape. This resulted in a surreal mix of strangers in town.

My personal loneliness, short staffing at work and, in all honesty, a sense of general misery now prevailed in my little world. If I had known, or even considered how the changing population dynamic would affect us in this small town, I am sure that we would have booked to go away. Maybe taking a trip to one of the major cities, like Melbourne, Sydney or Brisbane would have made our first Australian Christmas experience a more memorable and fulfilling experience.

This seasonal concoction of factors resulted in long hours for Nigel, with daytimes spent sleeping. Therefore, my new extra-curricular pastime was juggling full time shift work, keeping Jaime entertained and making sure Dave, our new puppy, was safe, amused and above all quiet. To say that this combination caused a strain on us was an understatement. The long Australian holidays, and missing the children in the UK so much, made emotions run high for both of us. At a time when it appeared everyone else was congregating with his or her families, we could not even find enough time for the three of us to spend quality family time together; it was too much to bear.

Was this what we came here for? I was unhappy, for the first time since we arrived, and I could not hide it from my closest friends at work. However, Nigel and I fell into the trap of keeping our feelings and emotions to ourselves, and sharing our troubles with only our friends, instead of each other. This was mainly due to us not having or not making enough quality time for each other together. This was a big mistake on both our parts. When we did have time together we spent it moaning, about each other and things we had or had not done etc. It was so stupid and negative, when I look back; however, at the time, when you are stuck in this vicious circle, you cannot see what you are doing to yourself. It felt like I was shutting down on all levels. I didn't even talk to Samantha and Robert about how I was feeling, which was unusual as we shared everything.

To everyone outside of Alice Springs, everything was fine, and happiness and normality prevailed, even when it did not. Something had to change. As our first year in Alice Springs ended, in addition to the already existing pressures, the influence of the Australian outback culture and mixing with people with very different values to ours, pulled at our relationship from many different angles. I know some people thought I was a snob; I sound like a snob sometimes. I feel that being brought up by my mum, a single parent, bringing up four girls on council housing estates in the UK, working two or three jobs at a time to survive, in no way qualifies me as a snob. However, compared to some in Alice Springs I looked and sounded like a posh English woman. One who did not know her place, as far as the many were concerned.

We had inadvertently become two separate people, instead of one strong unit. This made us weak as a family in a foreign country. Fortunately, for us, we had endured these kinds of pressures before, in the early years of our relationship. Consequently, we were able to spot the warning signs. Our love and mutual respect for one another was enough to awaken us to the imminent danger, making us realise that we had to make changes to our new lifestyle to prevent long-term damage. The realisation that the problems we were enduring were not a result of a problem with our relationship, but were resulting from the new cultural environment we now found ourselves in, was sad to acknowledge.

In Alice Springs, there were people who held a very low opinion of family, relationships and commitment. Our problem was finding the middle ground between fitting in with our work colleagues, and maintaining normal family life as we knew and loved it.

At one of our lowest points when there seemed to be no middle ground, a weekend away for Nigel in Darwin, and a girl's weekend in Melbourne for Jaime and I, made us both realise that now was the time for change. Sitting in the swimming pool with a glass of wine discussing our thoughts on how to move forward, we decided it was time for a commitment. So together, we set about planning our wedding.

Alice Springs performs its Christmas rituals in its own idiosyncratic way. The artificial Christmas tree, on the council lawns, perfectly shaped and decorated with hundreds of lights, which illuminate at dusk. Fake snow spray adorns shop windows that are selling t-shirts and accessories to cope with the extreme desert summer heat, which looks comical to those of us from the European contingent. At the hospital, there were varying degrees of festivity on display, ranging from Christmas trees on the wards to hand-made personalised gifts for the patients on Christmas day.

I elected to work the morning shift on Christmas day, so that we could celebrate in the afternoon, uninterrupted by work. The medical ward was as busy as ever, illness and disease stops for no one. However, it was a humbling experience to observe the cultural integration of staff and patients at this time of festive togetherness. It was unlike any Christmas day shift, I have worked in the UK. The level of appreciation for a good breakfast, a token gift and a festive lunch, even though some of the patients obviously had no comprehension of the true meaning of Christmas, was animated but heart-warming.

The staff on the medical ward went all out to ensure that everybody, staff and patients alike, enjoyed a piece of the Christmas merriment. The carol singers, going from ward to ward, headed up by the General Manager sporting her infamous bright red lipstick, evoked hand and thigh slapping, instead of the usual Christmas singalong, which was fascinating and entertaining all at the same time.

When I returned home, Nigel was preparing camel steaks and tiger prawns for the BBQ, and Jaime was waiting for me. Sitting with the pile of presents from friends and family abroad by the Christmas tree, seeing her sitting alone on Christmas day broke my heart. Holding back my tears, so that I did not upset her, I longed for her to have her brothers or sisters around to play guess 'what's in the present,' or to try to trick her into swaps of the least favourite item from their selection box. All of this made me feel guilty, for the first time, for bringing her here. Despite the Christmas CD, playing in the background, everything was quiet and felt very solemn. Nevertheless, Christmas had to go on for Jaime. Therefore, we pulled it together in true, positive Butfield style and she had a wonderful time. But we knew that this was not right. This was not Christmas; this was like reality television gone wrong.

We made a decision, that next year would be different; we had not come this far and endured so much, for Christmas and Alice Springs to bring us crashing down. Next year had to be different, or we would not make it here in Australia.

Chapter 9
"I do"

Despite Nigel and I having been together since 1997, for one reason or another we never got around to getting married. Initially, the problem was my ex-husband Jack. He would not agree to a divorce; he did not want me, but he did not want anyone else to have me either. Then, after a lot of legal wrangling when I was finally divorced, there never seemed to be the time or the money for such an extravagance, so we carried on as we were.

Was this decision subconsciously deliberate? We had both been married before, therefore were we protecting ourselves from enduring another marriage failure? We certainly did not lack commitment to each other, so was there really anything holding us back? Surely, you can always find a way; find the money, find the time for something you really want and believe in. Maybe it just did not seem important in the grand scheme of things at the time; however, the importance of marriage and that commitment was to become closer to my heart.

Within months of our arrival in Australia, our relationship endured some of its most strenuous testing. A new country, with a new culture gave us a new way of life, but new people with very different values to ours, pulled on our relationship from many different angles. In the later stages of 2008, in addition to the already existing pressures of 'separation anxiety' in relation to the children, the influence of Australian, outback culture made us realise that we already needed to make changes to our new lifestyle to prevent long-term damage to our relationship. This in part led to the realisation that we needed to re-affirm to each other our commitment to our relationship. At one of our lowest points, Nigel went on a trip to Darwin and returned with an engagement ring. Now, he had bought me an engagement ring before, in 2003, but we never did anything about getting married. This time was different. It felt different; it felt like the time was right. We had the time, the money and it could be our wedding, our way. Therefore, we set about making plans.

Our initial wedding location was to be on one of the Cook Islands, located in the middle of the South Pacific, between Tonga to the west and the Society Islands to the east. It was to have been a quiet affair, just the two of us, as it would not have been possible for all the children to come, unless we took at least another few years to plan and organise it! Then fate intervened again.

In April 2009, Nigel's mum, Sheila, was in the UK and during a routine health check-up an abdominal mass was detected. As Sheila endured several weeks of investigations, hospital consultations, and agonising waiting for results, Nigel was consumed with long-distance worrying, frustration and general feelings of helplessness. Longing for the results to be something benign, everyone's worst fears were confirmed when the mass turned out to be malignant liver metastasis, with an unknown primary and a poor prognosis. Without hesitation, we decided that we needed to visit Sheila in the UK, and after a lot of thought and hard talking we decided to bring the wedding forward, and change the location to the UK. It would still be our small perfect wedding, but we would marry in the UK so that Sheila could be there.

Gretna Green, Scotland is renowned as the place that couples elope, or run away to, when they want to marry, either without parental consent if they are young, or for a simpler style of wedding. Our rationale was simple; it was in the UK, easy to arrange and it was not a huge distance from where Sheila was staying. Our plans were then hastily made for our trip. One of the hardest decisions was whether or not Jaime should come with us. Trying to explain cancer to a child of any age is difficult, however Jaime and Sheila were very close, and we decided that we wanted Jaime to remember her as she was when she was last with us in Alice Springs. Therefore, we decided that Jaime would stay with Paul and Teresa while we were away.

We discussed our wedding plans with all of the children, and due to the time frames and relatively short notice involved, only Clair and Phillip would be able to accompany Sheila, Nigel and myself to Gretna Green. I felt really sad that Samantha and Robert would not be there, but we would be travelling down to Cornwall after the wedding to spend a week with them, so I had to make the best of this compromise.

We would leave on the 16th July, and our wedding date was set for 14th August 2009. As the date got closer, and Sheila's condition fluctuated, we wondered if she would be well enough to travel the few hours in the car to Scotland. However, she was a strong and determined woman and her wish to see Nigel married ignited an inner strength that powered her on.

Nigel was insistent that even though we were changing the wedding, it was still going to be our special day. He wanted me to be happy with everything we chose to do. Despite having been married twice before, I had never had the princess style, long wedding gown, so now was my chance. I bought my one and only, white wedding gown on eBay for the princely sum of sixty Australian dollars.

Nigel was perturbed by this. "It's a bit cheap. Are you sure, it's what you want? Why don't you fly to Melbourne and buy one from a proper wedding shop?" I love this man.

"Sweetheart, I really want this one; it's not about the money." We always call each other sweetheart, always have, one of those quirky romantic gestures from the early days that just stuck.

Anyway, I cannot say why exactly, but I fell in love with this strapless, white satin, mermaid style dress, with its silver-and-white sequined bodice, flattering ruched effect waist and large, perfectly formed bow supporting the chapel-length train. Good fortune was with me that day, because I spotted it just before the auction ended on eBay. Success, I won! I now had the first piece of my bridal outfit in place. EBay is a godsend to people in Alice Springs, especially if you need something special. There are a few specialist-clothing shops in Alice Springs for jeans, souvenir tee shirts, etc.; most everyday clothing comes from K-mart or Target. As almost everybody shops there at some point, trying to achieve an individual look can be challenging.

We booked the flights, hire car and various accommodations around the UK to facilitate visiting the children and other family during our visit. For our stay in Scotland, we found an apartment in the Cove Estate Manor House, near the King Robert the Bruce's cave, ancient monument. It is believed that King Robert the Bruce led his campaign to free Scotland after a period of isolation and despair in the cave. Coincidentally, it is also where the tale of the spider's behaviour in the web, enduring multiple knock backs, is believed to have instigated the saying, 'If at first you don't succeed try, try again.' It is ironic that one of our family mantras, which we have used in many circumstances over the years, originated from the place where we had now decided to marry. The need to be in Gretna Green for a few days prior to the wedding to submit paperwork, as we had organised the wedding from overseas, gave us the opportunity to visit some of the local area.

Nigel and Sheila had long shared a belief in Buddhist principles, and it seemed as if fate was intervening again when we found a leaflet for a Buddhist retreat and temple in our apartment. We decided to visit the temple the day after our arrival; it was a very spiritual and emotional experience. Kagyu Samye Ling was the first Tibetan Buddhist Centre in the western world. It is set in a tranquil valley on the banks of the River Esk. Two memories that particularly stand out for me from that day were firstly, 'The Cloutie Tree'.

The Cloutie tree forms part of Scottish and Tibetan tradition: the belief is that if you make a wish and attach one of the coloured pieces of cloth to the tree, over time as the cloth withers away the wish will be transported and one day that wish will be fulfilled. Following these instructions, we all took turns choosing and attaching ribbons to the tree. We all knew who, and what, we were all wishing for that day.

The second area that caused a few tears was the 'Prayer Wheel House'. Here you were encouraged to turn the prayer wheels as you pass, and make a silent prayer.

"The prayer wheels contain millions of mantras (short prayers) for peace and compassion, which have been written on blessed paper, which has been soaked in saffron water. Legend has it that as you turn the prayer wheel clockwise it activates the blessing of the mantras, releasing peace and compassion to the world." (http://samyeling.org)

It was a memorable day: Nigel, Clair and Sheila took some wonderful photographs in these serene settings, which will be treasured always.

The logistics of carrying the basic requirements for a wedding around the world in international luggage was no easy task. The full-length wedding gown, the artificial flower bouquet, tiara, wedding shoes, etc. was all in addition to everyday holiday clothes. It became the standing joke of the journey. We stayed in a hotel in Melbourne the night before our flight to London. That night, out came the wedding dress to 'hang' to avoid creases. Early next morning it was repacked, and this process continued when we arrived in UK until after our wedding day. Everywhere we stayed, my dress would hang in a different spot. In some places, where the wardrobe was too small, Nigel had to hang it from picture rails or curtain tracks.

When we arrived in Scotland a couple of days before the wedding, despite my best efforts, the dress was hugely creased. With Sheila's guidance, and Clair's assistance, we used blankets on the kitchen worktop to iron it, very carefully, for fear of scorching the various layers of the dress. Maybe a shorter, plainer dress had its merits after all! Nigel still had not organised or chosen his wedding outfit when we arrived in Scotland, therefore we went on a shopping trip to buy or hire suits for both him and Phillip. Suddenly they decided to go with traditional Scottish wedding paraphernalia. We ended up in the kilt hire shop, and spent a fun afternoon watching them try on the complete ensemble.

We then took Clair shopping for a dress to match the colour of the flowers in my bouquet. She found a beautiful purple cocktail dress, which fitted the occasion perfectly. This dress ended up adding humour to our wedding day, as we discovered when taking some photographs after the wedding. As we took shelter from the rain and adjusted our damp clothing, we found that Clair still had the security tag on her dress. For some reason this brought on another fit of hysterical laughter between me, Sheila and Clair. Probably because we had been so careful the night before checking everything for price tags and stickers, especially the bottom of our shoes, but had missed this large grey tag attached to Clair's dress lining. Nigel and Phillip, oblivious as to the cause of the hilarity, looked at us strangely.

On the 14th August 2009, we were married at The Forge, Gretna Green. It rained insidiously all day and the owner of the apartment loaned us large golfing umbrellas. We almost ran into the chapel, trying to avoid the puddles and heavy rain dirtying our wedding attire. Our neatly preened hair-dos were rain-and-wind swept, but it did not matter. As we stood in the chapel exchanging our vows my eyes welled up with tears, I could not stop crying. Tissues were passed discreetly, along with quiet, concerned whispers of, "are you alright?" The celebrant and a puzzled looking Nigel appeared quite concerned. Nigel looked me straight in the eyes and held my hands tightly as he mouthed, "I love you". At that moment, I knew that this time my marriage was for keeps. However, once I had composed myself I realised Nigel was sniggering, this then turned to laughing. He was laughing at me. Then I started laughing, and the poor wedding celebrant looked quite bemused, as tears turned to laughter: he wasn't sure why or what had caused it.

Having recovered from the emotional outbursts during the ceremony, the celebrant came with us to complete the signing of the register. Now, for all of those women reading this who are over the age of forty and who have had a child or four, you will know that parts of your anatomy can start to droop in a southerly direction at this time in your life. Yes, I am talking about my breasts. As I sat at the small wooden desk, my strapless wedding dress was gaping cavernously, as the boned corset became wedged on the arm of the carver style chair on which I was perched. As the celebrant leant over to show us where to sign, I think he got quite an eyeful; so much, so that he gestured to me to pull up my dress. Nigel thought this was hilarious, as did Clair and Phillip. I was mortified.

Gretna Green 14th August 2009
Sarah Jane, Nigel, Sheila and Phillip

The photographs and memories of that trip will stay with us forever. It was a turning point for us as we both realised that life has no guarantees. None of us knows how long we have on this planet, and we should live each day to the fullest, 'carpe diem' – 'seize the day.' Now was the time to say, "I do," not only to each other, but also to life.

This visit to the UK included another tearful reunion. Over a family dinner at 'Sloppy Joe's' in Colchester, Molly had agreed to attend and see me for the first time since the court proceedings. Due to her father's interference in our relationship, this was our first proper meeting in several years: A long -awaited mother and daughter reunion. I knew that in the past he had persuaded her that she did not need me in her life. He referred to me as Cruella de Vil, from the film, 'One Hundred and One Dalmatians,' when she was younger. Therefore, she would either called me Cruella, or Sarah, but not mum or mummy. This small gesture hurt more than I can ever put into words. Mere words do not do justice to the pain. It was as if a piece of me had been stolen. They say words cannot hurt you, but I disagree. Words, once said, cannot be taken back. Instead, they fester in your memory, a lingering reminder of the hurt, pain and betrayal. I loved her with every piece of me and the absence made that stronger, not weaker.

We were already in the restaurant with some of the other children, chatting and looking at the menus. I eagerly watched every movement of the glass entrance door. A part of me could not find my usual positivity: I could not bring myself to hope or believe that she really would come. I had been let down so many times in the past. Promised visits and holidays denied at the last moment, and with every betrayal, my heart broke a little more. I had convinced myself that Jack would persuade her against coming, even though she was now fifteen and a determined, strong-willed young woman, as I had witnessed by viewing her Facebook page.

Molly had asked if she could bring a friend to the meal, to which we readily agreed; after so much time this was going to be difficult for everyone so a new face at the table was a good idea. I glanced up from the menu and saw a striking red cardigan, with jet-black hair resting on the shoulders of a small-framed female figure. In the dimly-lit restaurant, I strained to see if it was Molly. Two people walked along the hallway to the restaurant. It was Molly. My heart did not just skip a beat; it beat so hard and so fast, that it felt like my chest would burst open. I was in some form of shock, unable to move. Nigel gave me a gentle nudge and I stood to attention awkwardly. Our eyes met and I sensed I was crying already. As I walked over to her, the time that had passed without seeing her was now immaterial. We were holding each other, a mother holding her daughter in her arms. My world stopped turning and I wanted this moment to last forever.

As mascara trailed down her face, we interrupted our embrace to visit the ladies' toilets, instead of heading directly back to the table. We hugged and cried: no words were necessary. I was holding my baby girl in my arms, not under the watchful eye of Jack, alone in the toilet of an American diner. Looking in the mirror we soon realised both of us had tear-trailed, mascara-stained faces, and we did our best with hand towels and liquid soap to regain some degree of facial touch up before deciding to rejoin the others.

We chatted like long lost friends, catching up on each other's news. The time and the distance that had been between us seemed a distant memory. The other children treated Molly and her friend, Liz, as if it was just another meeting of our big family. They chatted about all sorts, college choices, boyfriends, mopeds and, more importantly, who could eat the biggest burger on the menu. It was just like old times when they were younger, lots of laughing, banter and togetherness.

Nobody mentioned Jack. As the end of the evening crept up on us, I knew the dreaded goodbye was within sight. However, these few precious hours with Molly had been a perfect gift from God and I would not be greedy for more. The goodbye was tearful: Molly had photographs taken with the other children outside the restaurant, and then she and Liz left to get their bus. They did not want a lift home, and we did not force the issue. Molly said she would be in touch and I had to accept that.

While we were still in the UK she sent me a text to ask if we were visiting Colchester again before we left. I said we would be dropping Clair and Phil home after the holiday, and we agreed to meet up in Castle Park. One last embrace: Nigel took a wonderful photograph of the two of us, which I will always treasure. Especially now: as I write this four years on, we are yet again estranged, but more of that later in the book.

Overall, it was a bittersweet experience. Undoubtedly, the biggest sadness was the underlying knowledge that this would probably be the last time we would see Sheila. Anyone who has ever experienced the loss of parent will be able to empathise with some of what Nigel was feeling. We spent a lot of time during this visit debating if we should stay longer or if Nigel should stay on and I should go back to Jaime, etc. With the awful reality facing us, that no time frame can be put on the disease process, our reality was that Jaime was in Alice Springs, we both had jobs and commitments to return to, and more importantly, Sheila hated people fussing about her. She was 'old school,' not wanting to be a burden to anyone, and always had a 'carry on regardless' attitude, which Nigel knew and respected. Therefore, it was for these reasons that we upheld her wish that we should return to Australia as planned.

As our visit ended, Nigel said, the inevitable, final goodbye. Having lost my mother in my early twenties, I knew that the impending loss he would experience would stay with him always. Therefore, I would be there ready to support him every step of the way.

Chapter 10
Work the plan, to achieve your dream

Our plans towards eventually moving to our dream destination of Queensland were working, maybe not as smoothly as we had hoped, but nevertheless our new life felt good. We had both worked long and hard, on the temporary 457 visa, between January and September 2008, so that when our permanent residency came through, we were ready with $20,000 deposit and pre-approved mortgage to buy our first home together. This was a huge milestone and a very special achievement for us, as we would never have been able to afford to buy a property in the UK. In September 2008, on the advice of a recommended real estate agent, we bought the best house that we could afford, as he assured us that the value would increase even if we did no improvement work to it. This plan of action would eventually help us to raise the money we needed to buy a property in Queensland, where the prices were considerably lower.

One of the financial benefits of living and working in the Northern Territory, and in particular Alice Springs, is the lucrative property market and first time buyer incentives. Property in Alice Springs, of all types, is a valuable asset. The transient workforce means that for the short-and-long- term temporary work contracts, rental property is in high demand; and for workers recruited on permanent contracts property to buy is essential as renting long-term, after your relocation benefits package ceases, would not be financially worthwhile. We were so excited on the day that we took possession of our new home, in a quiet cul-de-sac in the suburb of Sadadeen. A three-bedroom, detached, single storey house, with a large above-ground swimming pool, garage, entertaining areas and gardens to the front and rear of the property.

A year later in September 2009, we were selling it for $475,000, which was $100,000 more than we had paid for it. I love it when a plan comes together. We repaid the mortgage, and after paying fees and taxes, we had enough money for a deposit on a small investment property in Alice Springs. For stage two of the plan, we would make a cash purchase of a piece of woodland in rural Queensland, on which we would build a log cabin or kit home for weekends away and holidays. One of the things that we love about Australia is the ability to take a road trip. There are so many great routes to explore, as you cross from state to state, or do 'the loop,' as many of the grey nomads embark on in their retirement. Another bonus to the grey nomads, on 'the loop,' is that while travelling, they can work the harvest trail – fruit and vegetable picking - to top up their superannuation/pension payments.

We had lined up two plots of land to view in Millmerran Woods, in the Darling Downs, Queensland. The small town of Millmerran, is approximately an hour away from Toowoomba to the east, and an hour away from Goondiwindi to the west. The routes to Queensland from the Northern Territory offer you a few choices. With hindsight, we placed far too much faith in the internet, and are the first to admit that on this particular adventure we were irresponsible and reckless in our choice of route. However, we strongly believe that life is for living and learning, and as you learn from your mistakes, we have no regrets.

The lesson being: searching for the shortest route is not necessarily the quickest or the safest method of choice. In our excited naivety, we chose the Plenty Highway, which we later found out was neither safe nor advisable to travel in a lone vehicle. The Plenty Highway is, in the main, an unsealed rough track between Queensland and the Northern Territory. The highway spans approximately 900 km's and, but for the driving conditions, it would the shortest route if you were travelling from Brisbane to Alice Springs. It takes you through an isolated part Australia where care and caution are advised. This said, we took our first Queensland road trip on this route, and for all of its adrenaline fuelled moments it was one of our most memorable adventures in Australia.

Corrugated road surface

Why it is unsafe? Firstly, there is the fact that there is no mobile telephone reception for the majority of the route, meaning that you should carry a satellite telephone. We could not afford a satellite telephone, although Nigel did invest in an UHF radio set, so that we at least had a chance of contacting a nearby trucker or outback ranch operating on one of the frequencies. Secondly, there is a high risk of damage to your vehicle, from kangaroos and other nocturnal wildlife from dusk until dawn, hence the advice not to drive overnight. As we were planning, quite irresponsibly again, to complete this round trip between Friday at 4 p.m. and Sunday evening, this would inevitably involve overnight driving. Thirdly, the internet search results tell you that there are two fuel stops on this route. However, it does not tell you that they only open for business when they have fuel, and even then, only if they feel like it.

Obviously, having lived in Alice Springs for a year, we already knew that on any trip out of town, even for a short drive, you always take drinking water, and water for the car in case of overheating. Therefore, we were prepared with plenty of water, ample food and luckily, a full fuel can. What more could we possibly need? We set off after Jaime came home from school, and we had both finished work on the Friday afternoon. Initially we headed an hour's drive north, along the North Stuart Highway, before turning off onto the Plenty Highway. We were to find out quickly that this was not the type of road we were expecting, and the word 'track' does not even begin to describe its condition.

Despite travelling in our four-wheel drive Nissan Pathfinder, the corrugated road surface constantly dragged and caused our vehicle to drift sideways, unless we kept at the exact, not too fast and not to slow speed, to keep the tyre pressures aligned. The ideal speed makes the car 'float' above the corrugated surface. If you can imagine driving over a corrugated tin roof, well that is what it looks and feels like. In addition, we were travelling over rocks the size of a man's fist, some with sharp edges, so the potential for tyre damage was high. A momentary lapse in concentration could be a disaster. These driving conditions placed a huge strain on both Nigel, as the driver, and me as the passenger. Despite being excited, we were both tired from a full day at work, and knowing what a tight schedule we had set for ourselves, we needed everything to run smoothly. We sang songs, talked about all sorts of trivia, ate snacks, drank cold drinks from our in-car fridge, and did almost anything to stay stimulated and awake. However, the heat made our tired eyes sore and as we knew that to conserve fuel we could not have the air con on for too long, we endured having the windows partly open, meaning we were terrorised by mosquitoes. In addition, we had Jaime to consider: although she was happy enough with her Nintendo games console and her array of jellied sweets in the back seat, this was not a normal journey.

In the desert, it gets dark quickly and after only a couple of hours driving, we were in darkness. It is still surprising how easy it is to get used to a background level of 'night light' living in suburbia. Often it is not until you leave the comfort and safety of light pollution, and you have to stop to go to the toilet or to clean the headlights, that you realize your headlights or a torch is the only thing between you and total darkness. There was the smallest section of the moon that I can ever recall, just when we needed a full moon; however, the stars in the desert are a magical sight and shooting stars are easily spotted. When you have the time to stop and stare, it can be like waiting for fireworks to go off on Bonfire night. It is captivating, a true spectacle of nature.

Some of the other perils of the darkness are firstly the potholes; the car suddenly unearths them without warning, causing the car and its contents to plunge down and then up, as everything in the car including us goes into a state of motion. CD's fly out of the rack, the mobile phone holder forgets its role, ends up in the foot well with the mobile phone. The car fridge bounces off its platform as Jaime's head hits the roof, as she is already seated high due to sitting on bedding and pillows. Just as you regain some degree of composure, you hit another one, and the process continues, exhaustingly. Secondly, in the darkness you do not know who or what could be lurking or prowling around. There are families and groups of people who live 'out bush' in terrain that would appear uninhabited. In the undergrowth, other inhabitants await unsuspecting visitors: scorpions, snakes and spiders, many of which are venomous, and a bite from some species would need more than a first aid kit. There is little to save you in the middle of the desert, with no means of summoning assistance. Therefore, the last thing you need in this setting is a puncture. Hearing that familiar thud as the deflated tyre makes a revolution on the corrugated road surface made us look at each other with that look of, 'Not now…. Please God, not now!'

"Don't worry we have a spare," Nigel said reassuringly as Jaime woke from her travelling slumber. "Just hold the torch. We will be on the road again in no time."

Famous last words: I stood, holding the torch as Nigel loosened the wheel-nuts and placed the jack under the vehicle, his tell-tale look towards the heavens told me all was not going to plan.

"We need a piece of wood; the jack doesn't go high enough." Laughingly, he said, "A piece of two by four would be good."

I could feel my head shaking, as my heart rate increased. I struggled to see any humour in the situation, as my brain said, 'fat chance, look where we are. No houses for hundreds of kilometres and you expect me to find something like that'.

I turned, as if to look, in what I knew would be a fruitless task, and the torch turned with me. Nigel shouted, "Hey, I need the light here."

As I turned back he yelled, "stop!" I froze, keeping as still as I could although shaking with fear, expecting that Nigel had spotted a snake or scorpion approaching my light. As the light from the torch shone on the uneven, corrugated road surface there, as if placed for exactly this type of roadside emergency, is a piece of wood, if not exactly, as near as damn it two by four. Nigel picked it up and hysterical laughter ensured. A gift from the gods, divine intervention or just bloody good luck, that piece of wood helped us to get the spare wheel on and we were trucking again.

In his cautionary tone, Nigel ever the practical realist said, "Let's hope that's our one and only puncture before we get to civilisation, because we only carry one spare."

You can imagine the tension from there onwards, as our journey continued, with us hoping and praying that we do not hit or scrape any of the tyres for the remainder of the Plenty Highway. Eventually we needed some sleep, or at least a power nap. We pulled over; the air is hot despite it being the early hours of the morning, and we played window games as we toyed with the various options. Windows open and we would be eaten by mosquitoes or risk that Huntsman spiders would crawl in, or windows up and melt in the tin box sauna we would create. We play with half measures and eventually decided it was probably better to keep driving with the air con on intermittently to conserve fuel.

As we started to pull away the sensation of someone or something watching us sent a tingle down our spines as a sparkle of light, about three or four feet from the ground caught our eyes. We both rubbed our eyes, thinking tiredness and hallucinations had set in. As the sparkling lights increased we realised it was a herd of cattle staring in at us, our lights reflecting from their eyes. They were completely unperturbed by the car noise as they surrounded us. The use of the horn eventually startled a few of them, enough for them to follow each other and make way for us to move forward. We looked at each other again. What had we got ourselves into this time?

Arriving and surviving the cross-country track adventure, the weird yet soothing sensation as we finally exit the 4x4 track and begin driving on tarmac earned a sigh of relief. We arrived in Winton, Queensland at daybreak and knew that we needed to park up, get some sleep. Besides the need for rest we had to wait for Tuff Tyres to open so that we could replace the punctured tyre, before we set off to Millmerran, which was still over 700 km's away, to view the two plots of land as arranged. Luckily for us the remainder of the journey to Millmerran was uneventful, as far as journeys go, and as we drove through the Queensland countryside and neared Millmerran Woods a sense of what can only be described as 'coming home' overwhelmed both of us. We had never been here before and had only viewed the locality on the internet, but it was unpretentious and homely. Maybe it was a throwback to my childhood, brought up in the Suffolk countryside; I am not sure, but whatever it was, it felt good.

The first piece of woodland was in Primrose Drive, which sounds like it could be a small road on a housing estate. This was one long, straight road with trees as far as the eye can see. In the distance, on some of the plots, you could make out the shape of houses and construction deep in the undergrowth. This is what we aspired to achieve. A log cabin, set well back in twenty acres of woodland. We could create our woodland retreat, which would be a place to escape from the rat race. The Primrose Drive plot had a partially cleared driveway and as we explored further there was evidence of previous inhabitants, who had made a start at clearing an area for a dwelling. There were pieces of construction material abandoned and piles of excavated earth. We loved the feel of the woods and the quietness.

The second piece of land was in Iron Bark Drive. The road to this piece of woodland was tarmac until about half a kilometre from the entrance. This factor meant this piece of woodland had a slightly lower value, having an unmade road to the front of it. There was no evidence of previous inhabitants and no apparent clearing: we knew this piece of woodland was the one that we wanted. Untouched, it was waiting to be nurtured. It must be a primitive perception, but the sensation of walking on land that showed no signs of any human ever having been there made me feel like an intrepid explorer. My proposed new territory was untouched by humans, although with plenty of evidence of its animal inhabitants. Noises, smells, hoof imprints and even snake trails, laid before me, but suddenly I was not scared of this; I was excited. As we looked to the right there was a large kangaroo staring right at us, and a huge goanna sunbathing on a fallen tree. They were initially still, and then moved off at a leisurely pace as we invaded 'their' patch.

Walking back to the car, we chatted like excitable children. How far into the woodland, would we make a clearing for the log cabin? Where would we build a dam for our water and maybe a secondary cabin for Jaime who would soon be too old to want to share with the parents? Endless questions and possibilities. We were happy, and once in the car, I called the agent and made an offer on the land. Within half hour, we got the call that our offer had been accepted. Stage two, subject to contract; we were going to be the very proud owners of twenty acres of woodland with permission to build a single-storey dwelling. It was coming together, and the dramas of the journey to get here were now a distant memory.

On the drive back, which was not on the Plenty Highway, but on the longer, more conventional route via Mount Isa, our conversations were consumed by plans, projections, and timeframes for progress visits, construction, etc. We were on our way to another new challenge: building a log cabin from scratch to our specifications. Life was good. We were not daunted or afraid of the work required to fulfil this aspect of our grand plan. This piece of land would also be the security for our future new family home in Queensland, which we anticipated buying in December 2009. Work the plan, to achieve your dream - our mantra continued.

Chapter 11
Grieving Bushman

Whether intentionally or not, we all take things for granted. It is often not until we lose someone precious that we question not only our own mortality, but also the purpose and meaning of our own life. The death of Sheila in October 2009, just two months after our visit, was devastating for Nigel. They had a close, mother and son relationship, even if it was sometimes difficult. One shared trait that they had was that they were both nomadic, free-spirited individuals who always harboured thoughts of wanting better. When we decided to move to Australia in 2008, Sheila applied for a one-year tourist visa, to come and live in Alice Springs to be near to Nigel, and us as a family, to see if she would like to live in Australia.

Sheila and I had always had a lot in common; our nursing backgrounds, sewing, a love of gardening and even the genre of books that we read, but most importantly our love for Nigel. Although we knew the prognosis of her cancer, when we had last seen Sheila in the UK, it was still an immense, devastating shock, when we received the dreaded telephone call. It was three o'clock in the morning when Nigel's brother, Richard, who was visiting his mum in the UK from New Zealand, called to say that she has passed away peacefully in the hospice. Nigel had spoken to Sheila on the hospice portable telephone less than forty-eight hours earlier, not knowing that it would be the last time mother and son would speak to one another.

After the call I had asked Nigel how she was and he said, "she was a little incoherent, and not herself." I think he could tell she was in pain, and the helplessness and despair of the situation descended on him again. Does human nature will you to stay positive and believe in miracles, even when your head and heart knows that it is too late? What is it about the knowledge of such a distressing, yet inevitable event, which still causes instant denial when it is finally revealed? Whatever you believe, and however each of us deals with these events in our lives, one thing is for certain: the truism, time is a great healer, is of no consolation at that moment of intense, all-consuming grief.

It quickly became obvious, in the early days and weeks of his grief, that Nigel needed to be alone. I wanted to support and help him; however, some life changing events have to be worked through, at your own pace, in your own way, alone with your thoughts and memories and definitely outside of a place like Alice Springs. Nigel developed an immediate zero tolerance, for people, noise, anything or anybody. I can only portray my observations of his mood, manner and ability to function as human being during this period, because only he truly knew the intensity of his pain. He was working at the Alice Springs Correctional Centre as a trainee prison officer at the time, and despite a few days compassionate leave, the early signs were there that more time was needed. The grieving process he needed to undertake was a necessity, because failure to cope in the prison environment would have compromised his ability to perform in such an arduous role, and could have endangered not only him, but also his colleagues.

It had already been discussed and agreed, before Sheila died, that we would not travel back to the UK for the funeral. In the early weeks that followed, as Nigel's response to his grief worsened, we decided that as the sale of our house was about to complete, there was no point Jaime and I moving into our investment house alone. We could not do the work it required without Nigel's input, and moving into and renovating a new property was in the' too hard basket,' given the circumstances; therefore we needed to change our plans slightly. Our new, revised plan of action was that Nigel would go and live alone in our twenty acres of woodland, in Millmerran, Queensland. Jaime and I would live in a small, rented apartment in Alice Springs and we would rent out the investment unit on a flexible lease in its current condition, for a lower rent. This would enable us to survive on one income, and we could then let time and grief take its course.

Nigel and the boys have a new home in the woods

For Nigel, living a solitary existence in the woods would not only give him time to think, remember and evaluate, but also it was the perfect distraction. This piece of woodland was to be our future idyllic retreat. Our new project needed him, just as he needed solitude. He could spend time there, getting to know and appreciate the land, and its idiosyncrasies: the wildlife, the climate and the way the rain flows through the naturally-formed tracks to name but a few.

Jaime and I moved to St Stephen's Road, just over a kilometre from the hospital. As Nigel had taken the family car with him, my friend, Carol, would either lend me her car, or drive us if we needed to get heavy shopping, or Jaime needed to go to a friend's house that was not in walking distance. Our furniture and belongings went into storage and Nigel set off with the trailer, a tent, and camping equipment, and of course Dave and Buster, his only companions, offering their unconditional love and affection.

Since February 2009, I had been working as Clinical Nurse Manager on the new Continuing Care Unit. This meant I was working regular hours, Monday to Friday, with no shift-work. Jaime and I soon developed a new routine; meeting up after work, and school, having a swim at the town pool followed by some girlie shopping or coffee time, before making our way home to have our one-hour telephone call with Nigel, to catch up on the day's events. However, more importantly, the calls enabled me to keep a close check on his mental health. Although isolation gave Nigel many positives, the reality was that I was a three-hour flight away, and I needed to be ever conscious of the risks, of dealing with my grief-stricken husband via telephone calls, Skype and letters.

With this in mind, it was important to have a visit organised: for Jaime and I to visit him and 'our boys.' Therefore, we planned a four-day, long weekend for six weeks after he had left Alice Springs. We booked flights with Tiger Airways from Alice Springs to Brisbane. Nigel would pick us up at the airport and take us to Millmerran to stay for two nights in the woods, before spending the final two nights in an apartment in Brisbane. This was important, because isolation has to be balanced with reality, and a small dose of the real world, as a family, having a city break before Jaime and I returned to Alice Springs, was perfect.

It was amazing to see him again. Even though it had only been six weeks, the improvement in both his physical and mental health was obvious. He was more relaxed, less anxious: he had spent time putting his thoughts down on paper, and had started to work on positive ways to deal with his loss. Sheila had been a hugely important part of his life, and this void needed to be acknowledged, without pushing her memory aside. During his time alone in the woods, having started out with just a tent and a torch, he had managed to create a clearing and buy an old caravan, which had then become his home. He filled his days with cutting down trees, and clearing the undergrowth to make the space for our new woodland retreat.

Nigel is a very private person, and keeps a lot of his emotions and feelings to himself. However, he did confide in me that the solitude and isolation gave him the opportunity to cry as loud as wanted; shout, scream and generally take out his frustrations on the trees, cutting, clearing and sawing wood. This freedom to express his grief would not have been available to him in Alice Springs. Dave and Buster were with him through these trying times, to comfort him, reassure him and love him, and he still often says, "thank God for those boys".

During our brief visit, Nigel showed us the area of woodland he had mapped out for our wood cabin to be erected, the area to have the dam dug, and the various areas for seating and shelter in the future. Jaime and I helped with his current project, which was clearing trees and undergrowth, to make a driveway that would be suitable for vehicles and other equipment in the future. It was hot, tiring but strangely exhilarating work. We worked as a team; the signs were there that the normality of family life was achievable and that the time alone in our woodland retreat was working for him.

It was quite a shock to the system to experience the humidity of Queensland, after the dry heat of Alice Springs. The humidity, in conjunction with the heat, saps you after a very limited period of physical exertion, therefore to achieve any real progress, you have to start early at first light, and then utilise the shade in the afternoon for less physical pursuits. The time seemed to go so fast, but to sit and talk with only the birds, kangaroos, wallabies and insects to interrupt you, was idyllic. Jaime spent hours exploring, making tree houses and generally enjoying the outdoors: she loved the freedom.

In readiness for our city break, we settled Dave and Buster at the local kennels, near Millmerran, and set off on our drive to New Farm, Brisbane. We had booked in for two nights at the Allender Apartments, which are walking distance to the main thoroughfare of Brunswick Street. This area has a host of excellent restaurants, cafes' and specialist shops. Brunswick Street meets Merthyr Road, in an area known as Merthyr Village, with even more good food and coffee. We walked these streets sampling many delights. The James Street precinct, just minutes away, has fresh fish and produce markets, an art-house cinema and several upmarket bars and cafes.

New Farm is an inner Brisbane suburb, situated on the bend of the Brisbane River located two kilometres from the CBD. The name, New Farm, derived from the farming history of the area, is better known as Brisbane's "Little Italy," as many Italian immigrants initially settled there. It is a beautiful, cosmopolitan area with the western side characterised by large houses, and tree-lined streets. The historic New

Farm Park, situated at the south-eastern end of the peninsula, boasts magnificent gardens, Jacaranda and fig trees. The area is home to a mix of interesting, historic and modern features, including the former electric tramway power station to the east, which has been regenerated into a community arts and performance hub. 'The Powerhouse,' as it is known, hosts thought-provoking exhibitions, concerts and recitals.

We took advantage of many of these attractions, and savoured delightfully aromatic coffee at various small cafés, nestled amongst vintage shops and restaurants. We ate, drank and, most importantly, we talked planning for our future. The future was now the key to bringing my grieving bushman back to the real world. After a great deal of discussion we decided to arrange to move into our investment property, to start the renovations, and that Nigel would return to Alice Springs in four weeks' time. We planned to see out the remainder of our two-year visa time as planned in Alice Springs, with visits scheduled to start the work on our retreat in the woods, before making a permanent move to Queensland.

When Nigel returned to Alice Springs, he did not return to work at the prison. Instead, he went back to his roots as a taxi-driver, and began work for a private hire cab company. He loves driving, and it was the perfect way to achieve earning money for our plans, and to give him a sense of purpose, with less stress and anxiety. The working hours meant we had lots of time together, as a couple and a family. The healing process was in place: 'time' was working.

Within a few weeks of his return, it was Christmas 2009. Another Christmas in Alice Springs: would this be deja vu? Despite, what we said last Christmas, circumstances meant we were spending Christmas in here again. Some things had changed, but it was another Christmas with just the three of us. However, as always trying to put the positive spin on this situation, we knew that it was part of our longer-term plan and therefore this short-term sacrifice was for our long-term gain.

Living in our two-bedroom unit, near the telegraph station, we were busy replacing the bathroom, decorating and generally making it ready for tenants in a few months' time, when we hoped to be moving to Queensland.

With Nigel no longer working at the prison or as a bouncer, we had much more time together over this Christmas period to plan our future. We were searching the internet for our next project, a renovation property in Queensland. We found the ideal property. A high set house, on a corner plot, with three bedrooms and the potential to convert the vacant space under the house into a guest flat, for the children when they visit. We viewed photographs and information, sent from friends and trades people who viewed on our behalf. Quotes for work that we would not be able to complete ourselves were obtained, and it was 'all good' as they say in Australia.

In the week between Christmas and New Year, our offer was accepted subject to surveys and legal searches. With the finance already in place from the bank, the sale went through seamlessly. Excitedly, we planned our first trip to start work on the house at Easter when my annual leave was booked. Knowing that next year, Christmas 2010, we would be in the UK preparing for Samantha and Doug's wedding, on 11th January 2011, we knew that whatever happened, we had spent our last Christmas in Alice Springs. That was a great feeling.

Moving on to a new chapter now felt more real, and our Australian adventure was developing, albeit with a few hiccups, into the lifestyle of which we had dreamed. A goal, a purpose, a focus of all our energies proved the perfect follow up to the healing time Nigel had spent in the woods.

Chapter 12
Family Health tested

As part of the immigration visa process, we had all undergone intensive medicals, x-rays and blood tests. With all of us given a full medical clearance, we moved safe in the knowledge that at least we were healthy.

Within the first three months of commencing my employment at Alice Springs Hospital, the screening continued, due to the increased risk of tuberculosis (TB). In the Northern Territory, the heightened risk of TB, in addition to acute and chronic disease, means that employment health screenings are rigorous and proactive. TB is heavily associated with poverty, overcrowding, and poor nutrition, therefore it is common in aboriginal, indigenous communities like Alice Springs. TB is essentially a lung infection. Inhalation of the bacterium, Mycobacterium tuberculosis, can infiltrate the lungs and grow, forming wart-like lumps, potentially causing symptoms such as productive cough, weight loss and loss of appetite.

I attended for my routine Mantoux Tuberculin Skin Test, (TST) as a preventative measure; screening is provided for workers in high risk areas, i.e. people exposed to TB as a result of their job, like healthcare workers. The TST involves injecting a tiny amount of tuberculin purified protein derivative into the skin tissue just below the surface on the inner aspect of the forearm, producing a pale coloured wheal or swollen area, of up to 10 mm in diameter. My appointment was booked to return to the clinic in one week, to assess the site for signs of a reaction and the measurement of my reaction, if any. I noticed immediately that my wheal was not pale, as the nurse and the information leaflet had led me to expect. It was very red and swelling quickly. On the medical ward, during my shift later that day, one of the medical registrars had a look, and reassured me. The swelling and redness extended in length, which I knew was normal, but the height was concerning. However, it was not painful, so I waited. I remember sitting in the clinic, a week later, for my assessment and looking at my arm and thinking, 'I hope this is normal.'

When I walked into the clinical room, Tracey, the Clinical Nurse Specialist, looked at my arm, looked at me and rolled her eyes as she reached for her specially marked ruler. A red line on it marked the difference between a pass and a fail. As the ruler neared my skin, I already knew the result - I had failed. An immediate chest x-ray was needed to check for the presence of tubercles in my lungs. As it is possible to get a false, positive result on the TST test, I was not overly concerned. I telephoned the ward, to say I would be longer than planned at my appointment. Staff members at Alice Springs Hospital have all screening appointments in work time, so courtesy is expected if things overrun. Another benefit of being 'staff,' was that I did not have to wait in line for my x-ray. I was straight in, undressed, x-rayed and done. My only wait was in reception, to collect my developed x-ray films before returning to the clinic. This time it was the infectious disease registrar waiting to see me. As soon as the films went up on the x-ray box, even I could notice a difference from the x-ray taken just months earlier, for our visa medicals. Clusters of white were evident across both lungs.

It became evident that TB exposure had occurred, and that, as I was asymptomatic of the infection, it was probably latent TB. The treatment plan was that I should commence prophylactic (preventative) treatment immediately. It was likely that exposure to TB had occurred since my arrival in Alice Springs, as my visa x-ray had been clear. My treatment commenced; three tablets, once a day in the morning, with weekly checks with the infectious disease nurse, for signs of an adverse reaction to the treatment. I had the all clear to continue working, and reassurance was given that I was not putting Nigel or Jaime at risk, as only exposure to TB had occurred. Only exposure! Don't you love the short statements that are made, usually by those unaffected by what you are enduring? The advice with the treatment was to avoid alcohol, yeast and if possible, meat products. A strange combination, I thought, as I pondered the impact to my diet, as I do love my food and a nice glass of wine.

Avoiding alcohol is a standard precaution with most medications, so I dutifully adhered, but surely not bread and meat. As rebellious as ever, I attempted to eat bread and meat, and immediately realised why you might like to avoid them. Both tasted like aluminium foil in my mouth. I tried a variation of meats; white and red, it made no difference. That was it, I was now a medication-induced vegetarian! Bread, my staple diet since childhood, was a big loss, but not as big as the weight loss that occurred by dropping these three elements of my diet.

In six months, I went from 74 to 59 kilograms, my lowest ever-adult weight. It was amazing. Every week, I went for my check up, and weigh in; and each week as the number on the scales reduced, the better I felt.

The nurse would routinely ask, "Are you dieting?"

My reply, "No, but this is great".

The accidental weight loss gave me more energy, and a heightened sense of self-esteem. I could now wear shorts, bikinis or a skimpy singlet, with no lumps or bumps on show. The downside of the medication was the gastric side effects, an almost constant feeling of indigestion. This resulted in the need to take omeprazole, a drug used to reduce acid formation in the stomach, throughout the course of my treatment. When my weight dipped below sixty kilograms, a repeat x-ray to assess the ongoing need for my TB medication was requested. The difference was amazing: the white areas were gone, and my treatment was discontinued.

In some of the nursing roles in my career, I have taught weight management to patients, for a variety of medical reasons. However, no amount of education can prepare you for the difference in your mental state when you actually lose the weight. I had never been skinny, not even as a child; 'plump' was how I was described at school. Losing this amount of weight, in my forties, gave me a new-found confidence. I could wear clothes that fitted, and showed off my figure: ironically, it made me exercise more, because I now felt good wearing sportswear. A 'new me' developed. I changed my hairstyle and colour, my skin routine, my nails; pretty much everything. In that six month period, it was a total makeover. Nigel and my friends at work were amazed by the transformation.

My child, traumatised

I was not the only one to experience a health issue, during our time in Australia. Unfortunately, Jaime had her own experience, which sadly will now be part of her life forever. In April 2010, Jaime went on a school trip; it was for teenage girls to learn team-building skills. They went to a working outback cattle ranch, about two hours' drive from Alice Springs, to learn how to live, and work as a team. Their sleeping quarters were two raised bunks, and groundsheets, under a shade cloth. These outdoor living quarters would be home for ten days, teaching them about personal safety around wild animals, with dingoes visiting at night, as well as respect for animals of all varieties, both wild and domesticated. Jaime had the most amazing time at the camp, including bareback horse and cattle riding, horsemanship skills, campfire cooking and so much more. She returned with a more confident approach to daily life, and was willing to be part of a team again, something she had shied away from since her bullying experience at St Phillips College.

On her return, she had a boil on her right knee, so we took her to the doctor. She had a course of antibiotics, and within ten days it had healed, with just a red mark remaining. In the three weeks that followed, Jaime would sporadically complain of pain in her right groin, but with no lumps or redness present, in addition to the fact that she was a pubescent girl, period pains and cramps were blamed. In hindsight, this was a huge oversight on my part. When Jaime decided to pull out of a five km run, which she had been training for, it should have been a sign that something more serious was wrong. I live with that guilt to this day.

Two days later, she was getting ready for school when she suddenly started crying, and was obviously in excruciating pain. I examined her leg and groin again and was shocked to find red streaks, indicating infection in the lymph system from her right groin down her thigh, ending at her knee. Knowing immediately that infection was present; I rushed her to the emergency department. Luckily, again being a staff member, we went straight through to triage. After a hasty referral to the surgical team, and we were sent to the ultra sound scanning room so that they could investigate the origin of the infection. The problem was apparent immediately. As the ultrasound probe was gently moved over her groin, despite her screaming and writhing around in pain, an abscess, 5 cm by 3 cm in size, was detected. No wonder she was in so much pain. Jaime was immediately admitted to the children's ward, where again as a staff privilege, the ward manager made sure that we had a side room, so that I could stay with her. The decision was made to treat conservatively initially, with IV antibiotics and pain relief. For three long days, and nights, Jaime cried; the pain was uncontrollable, resulting in her being unable to move, walk or eat without distress. On the fourth day they scanned her again: the abscess had grown, and an emergency theatre slot was scheduled. Leaving Jaime, as they pushed her through from the anaesthetic room to the theatre was one of the hardest things. I wished it were me enduring this pain. I wished I could spare her this experience, but it was too late, my wishes could not come true. Nervously, as I waited in the theatre staff room, an anaesthetist who had assisted in sedating Jaime due to her distress came in and spoke to me. He treated me like a parent, and not a staff member, which I really appreciated, because this is one of the downsides of the staff privilege. When everyone knows you are a staff member, assumptions are made and consequently less is explained to you. However, at a time of immense emotional stress, as a mum you need that explanation, and reassurance, just as much as a layperson.

The surgery went as well as it could. The abscess was drained, and due to its size and the risk of infection, it would have to heal naturally from within. It could not be sutured, therefore it left a huge, gaping hole that was packed with ribbon gauze. That night she finally slept, rousing only slightly, when IV fluid bags were changed or IV analgesia was administered. I was confident the worst was over. How wrong I was. The following morning, as we awaited the surgical team rounds, the nurses were busy with the children who did not have parents in attendance. The surgeon and his entourage of medical students walked in, and began chatting. I walked to the door to see if the nurse was on her way with the dressing trolley. As I turned to look at Jaime, I saw the surgeon's hand reach for the wound packing: it was as if I was behind glass, unable to be heard.

I was shouting, "Stop no! Please God no!"

Instead of waiting for the nurse to return with the saline to soak the gauze pack before removal, he wrenched the pack out revealing raw bleeding tissue. Jaime was hysterical and uncontrollable. She leapt off the bed, blood spurting from the wound and the ripped out IV cannula sites. As I reached her, she had curled into the foetal position on the floor, shaking and screaming. Blood and serous fluid leaked down her legs, being absorbed by the hospital gown like beetroot juice soaking into white bread. The surgical team made a hasty exit, shouting orders for pain relief and assistance, while nurses rushed in around us. I cradled Jaime in my arms, rocking her like a baby, until they came with a morphine injection. I would not let them move her until it started to take effect. Alone, I gently lifted her onto the bed, where I laid holding her tightly. I never wanted to let her go again.

It took sedation, and many hours of comforting to get her to a stable condition. Unfortunately, the extreme pain she endured triggered a reaction in her brain, and ever since that time, whenever she experiences pain, anywhere in her body, she feels that pain in her right leg. The term for this condition is Complex Regional Pain Syndrome. (CRPS) The abscess site took five months to heal, with initially daily packing and dressing then changing to alternate days. A large scar remains; we jokingly call it her 'shark bite,' because for a girl who loved wearing bikinis, she can now only wear shorts for swimming. The scar is a constant reminder of a surgeon's thoughtlessness and presumption. The mental scar, which haunts her at times of weakness, is a continual reminder of the pain.

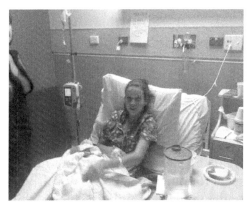

Jaime in Alice Springs Hospital 3 days after her operation

Since then Jaime has had a couple of hospital admissions for her CRPS in Queensland and Tasmania, and now as I write, also in the UK. Unfortunately for Jaime, people's ignorance of the condition causes her more distress than the pain, because sometimes she has no obvious cause of the intense pain she feels, which is triggering the relapse in her condition. We have undertaken physiotherapy, hydrotherapy, desensitization and cognitive behaviour sessions to help her, but ultimately the condition can exhibit itself at times of stress and physical pain, so she has to be prepared to live with this for the rest of her life. The positive from this horrendous ordeal, for Jaime and I, was that we shared every minute of the pain and anguish. I never left her bedside, in the hospital in Alice Springs or during the episodes since then. She is still developing the skills needed, as a young woman living away from home, to deal with a pain episode when I cannot be there. I am so proud of her, and our special bond that was formed during her suffering and personal adversity will remain always

.

Chapter 13
New beginnings in Queensland

Who would, or could have known, that what was to be the ultimate achievement of our Australian dream- to buy and renovate a house in Queensland - would be shaken to its core, before it had even begun. On the fourth day of our first visit to our newly acquired property in Ipswich, Queensland, we were the victims of an attack of road rage. An unkempt, dilapidated Ute rammed into our hire car; a middle-aged man, with no respect for other road users, was driving it. The word 'Ute,' is an Australian term for a utility vehicle, which usually consists of a two-door passenger cab with a cargo tray at the rear.

This threatened to halt our plans in their tracks. Although there was only minor physical damage to the car, the psychological effects of his threatening behaviour affected us much deeper as a family. Nigel was driving the hire car, and had noticed the Ute tailgating us from the first set of traffic lights in Jacaranda Street. He made a joke of how the driver must be hungry, and eager to get home for lunch. Nigel became increasingly concerned about how close he was getting and so he began slowing down to encourage the driver to pass. As we exited the slip road, towards the shopping village, the driver in the Ute rammed into the back of us. Nigel brought the car to a sudden halt and jumped out, just as the Ute was being reversed, ready to drive off from the scene of the accident. Nigel ran to the window of the drivers' side, which luckily was open, and pulled the keys out, the driver was verbally abusive, threatening, and grabbing at Nigel. The passenger in the Ute, a woman in her late fifties, got out in disgust and walked off. I was on the telephone to the police trying to give the registration details, not even sure of the name of the road we were in. I was fearful for Nigel's safety as he was in confrontation with the driver, and concerned for Jaime who did not understand what was happening, and was crying and sobbing uncontrollably.

Jaime, who was in the backseat of the car, when it was impacted, was distraught. She had witnessed the Ute tailgating us for a while before the impact, and said later that he had been making finger gestures to her/us. The image the Ute, so close behind us that at times it felt as if it was attached, that man's face so close as if he was in the car with us and Jaime screaming, in fear, still haunts me. This is offset by the kindness of a stranger who lifted her over the crash barrier to safety, once I got her out of the car. As for me, I was in the passenger seat facing the back, trying to reassure Jaime at the time of impact, and consequently suffered a whiplash injury. It was the psychological trauma of this incident which was most severe, however. In part, this was compounded by the unfeeling, sarcastic attitude of the female police officer who attended the scene. She treated us as if we were the ones at fault, that we made him do it, and consequently Nigel got into an altercation with her when he suggested that the Ute driver should be breath-tested.

The police officer's indignant reply, "Are you trying to tell me how to do my job?"

The aftermath of this resulted in me developing a form of post-traumatic stress disorder (PTSD) and driving anxiety. These conditions changed me as a person, changed my life and have taken away the independence and enjoyment of travel. I am still trying to combat my driving anxiety. This course of events would change our plans, time frames and me, as a nurse, wife and mother, for the foreseeable future. Although my whiplash injury was treated efficiently initially at the Ipswich Hospital, and subsequently by my GP, the stress and anxiety associated with the psychological impact was devastating. It appeared irrational, but I could not control it. I lost my confidence in everything. Now that sounds dramatic, like an overreaction; and it was, but I cannot describe it any other way. I took up walking to avoid needing the car. When I attempted to return to work I walked five kilometers each way, however, when I got there I could not function. I could not sleep due to flashbacks of the accident, and the sleep deprivation fuelled my fears of travel.

My doctor advised me to take sick leave during the counselling period. I spent six weeks trying to sit in the car for periods of five minutes, ten minutes, etc., and all the time monitoring my anxiety levels. Then the day came when I had to drive: I had no choice. Nigel was at work, and Carol was away; I had to get in the car. I had to drive to take Jaime her lunch, which she had forgotten, for a school trip. It took me over an hour to get in the car, and the thought of reversing out of the drive filled me with horror. It then all became a blur; suddenly I was driving, as if in autopilot. I knew I wanted to get this over and done with as quickly as possible. I remember making the lunch drop off: the next thing I knew a police officer was flagging me down on the North Stuart Highway.

As he approached the car, I was shaking so much I must have looked like I was having a seizure. I was one km from home; I had nearly made it. The irony is, that I was speeding, and I got my first and last speeding fine. I do not drive anymore. I was determined that there was nothing, or no-one that would stand in the way of our dream. Forever the optimist, we would make our next adventure a success whatever the obstacles or challenges. Therefore, despite the impact that the accident had on my ability to function as a human being, in the summer of 2010, I took all my annual leave and sick leave and eventually unpaid leave, to finish my contract at Alice Spring Hospital and we finally made the move to live in Queensland permanently.

Finally, we had made it. We had accepted the compromise, which was two years in Northern Territory, to achieve our dream of living in Queensland. Moving direct from the UK to Queensland would have taken longer to achieve initially, and at the time, we thought it would have been more arduous. Hindsight would have been a wonderful gift, and would have been an asset, but where is the fun in that? When we consider the path and the challenges we have faced getting from the UK to Alice Springs and finally to Queensland, we certainly did not end up taking the easy option.

Despite the challenges of our Australian adventure, the fact was that we had 'made it'. We had achieved moving to start a new life in our dream destination, Queensland, in a house that we were excited about renovating, and making into a 'home,' that all of our children would be able to visit, and stay in whenever they wanted, or needed to. It was our family home. There was a lot of work to do, and we knew that we were essentially starting over again. With new jobs needed, and the issue of my PTSD and driving anxiety hanging over us, we had to stay focused and positive as always.

Firstly, we had to move house. With new tenants, and a property agent managing our unit in Alice Springs, our interstate move was set, but once again fate intervened. Jaime's discharge from hospital was delayed, following her abscess surgery, as she had contracted a post-operative infection. With Jaime unfit to leave hospital, let alone travel, Nigel had to do the huge road trip from Alice Springs to Queensland alone - well, apart from the 'boys,' who always love a road trip.

Nigel and the boys on the way to Queensland alone!

We had rented out the unit furnished, and put some things in storage, but everything else was in a trailer, which would accompany Nigel on his journey. A reality check in hindsight: should we have taken these events as a sign that the move to Queensland was doomed from the start? We had already experienced the road rage car accident at Easter in Ipswich, and now this. Was the universe trying to tell us something? If it was, we did not listen.

A week later Jaime was fit to fly, and we eventually joined Nigel and the 'boys' in Ipswich. Jaime needed to convalesce, and apart from settling in, our priority was to establish a source of income. We had already discussed, researched and formulated a business plan for our new venture, and therefore knew exactly what we had to do. We based it on our experiences in Cornwall, where we had run a successful cleaning and gardening business called 'Spick 'n' Span'. We decided that this would be an ideal business opportunity in Queensland, too. We could work together, something which has always been successful for us, and we would have the flexibility to plan our business around our renovation schedule. I would not have to drive anywhere and I could work on rebuilding my confidence in all aspects of my life.

Within a few days, we had our photo identification name badges printed, and we had purchased the additional cleaning and gardening equipment we needed. The advertising and marketing on internet directories, and distributing door-to-door fliers, kept us busy, and by the end of week one, we had received six new enquiries, three of which converted to new customers: we were happy. Our four-wheel drive car and trailer were our new business vehicles, so Nigel was busy sorting out Queensland vehicle registrations, which was a more stringent process than it has been in the Northern Territory. Aside from this, I was also 'assistant wedding planner' for Samantha's wedding set for January 2011. There were many emails, pricing and searching for venues, accommodation, flights etc., going on besides our business promotion activities.

With our business set up, and with several bond cleans scheduled, we were busy. A bond clean is organised or completed by the tenant vacating a rental property, in order to have their deposit returned. However, our other focus was that we were arranging the first visit to Queensland in August for Molly, Clair and Phillip. Their first trip to see us in Australia, and we were so happy that it was to be to the new family home, even though it was a bit of building site in places! It would be their first long-haul flight, and their first flight without a parent accompanying them; it was rather daunting. This was a big step forward for my relationship with Molly. Since the tearful reunion in 2009, on our wedding trip to the UK, we had remained in contact and uncharacteristically Jack had not interfered. I was excited, nervous, but mostly so grateful that my prayers had been answered.

As new business leads were generated, we realised we had found a gap in the market for high quality bond cleans. Ironically, although compared to the UK, the standard of cleanliness in Australia is perceived by some people to be deficient, the requirement for perfection for departing tenants is higher than that in the UK, and a number of bond deposits are not returned in full. The weeks that followed were intense. We were cautious not to over commit with the business, but marketing and advertising had to be ongoing. The gardening side, for regular maintenance contracts, started to build and alongside that, weekly domestic cleans for busy professionals. We had made the decision that we were not growing a business to employ staff: we only wanted to be self-sustaining, earning enough to meet our own needs, not build an empire. We had been in that situation before, and the pressure and commitment would have detracted from the lifestyle we were looking for in Queensland.

Ipswich is approximately a forty-minute drive from Brisbane: it is home to numerous commuters, due to excellent train links, and the ever-evolving and improving road infrastructure. We had not lived in a built up, suburban area like this before; having gone from a sleepy market town in Cornwall, to the quiet suburbs of Alice Springs, and now to the city of Ipswich, only a couple of kilometres from the CBD. We therefore looked forward to our long weekend visits to our woodland in Millmerran, as an escape from city life. Following on from the work Nigel completed there at the end 2009, the prospect of building our log cabin became ever more exciting, as we researched the quotes and worked on marking out the plot ready for clearing.

Finally, the time had arrived for Molly, Clair and Phillip to arrive from the UK. We had planned a few days at the house in Ipswich, an overnight trip to the woods in Millmerran, so that they could see our project and hear first-hand what we hoped to achieve, and the finale of the visit would be family holiday to Cairns, North Queensland. We would be staying in the tropical rain forest resort of Kuranda, and there would be a variety of wildlife, beaches and a highly-anticipated whale watching tour. The time spent with the children in the various places was truly memorable. We had so many good times, and more laughter than was good for my abdominal muscles! We visited the Gold Coast, two hours' drive from Ipswich, and took them all to Movie World and Wet 'n' Wild. In Surfer's Paradise, they loved taking the iconic pictures to show their friends at home. However, it was the trip to Cairns, which allowed everyone to experience the Australian sea life, wildlife and climate at its best. Clair and Phillip still talk about that holiday today. Nigel is extremely close to Clair and Phillip, and their similarity in character and humour always promotes joking and face-twisting comedy when they are together.

From left to right: Molly, Sarah Jane, Jaime,
Clair and Phillip arriving in Cairns in Queensland

Bearing in mind the unstable relationship history between myself and Molly, prior to the holiday, it was nerve-racking to start with. However, the more time we spent together, and seeing her bond with Jaime, her true blood sister, was a mother's joy. Even if it was only temporary, as it transpired, because Jack returned to his old, manipulative tricks and my relationship with Molly became estranged once more when she went home to the UK.

With the holiday over, and struggling with the anti-climax and a degree of homesickness, not for the UK, but for the children, we focused on our business, and our woodland retreat project. We spent a great deal of time, and research, contemplating finding the financial resources to increase the pace of the project. The renovation of our house in Ipswich was going well, doing a lot of the work ourselves, and we were very pleased with the end result. A spacious family home, with three double bedrooms; an open plan kitchen dining room; and a large, lounge that opened into the sunroom, which enveloped the corner of the house, and therefore had sun through the tinted glass for the majority of the day. The house was light and airy, but something was missing for us. As we pondered this missing ingredient, we eventually realised it did not lack something at all. In fact, it actually had something which many find appealing and essential, but something which we did not enjoy: the proximity to city life.

From May to December 2010, we worked our plans to stabilise ourselves in Queensland. Our property in Alice Springs had increased in value, and our renovation of the house in Ipswich was complete. However, something still did not feel right. We loved our house in Ipswich, and the renovation work we had done to it, turning it from an unloved house into a family home. We loved the garden and entertaining area we had created, and if we could have picked up the house and transplanted it into somewhere quieter, then life would have been perfect.

We decided to put the house in Alice Springs on the market, even though we were still undecided about our dilemma with the house in Ipswich. We felt a strong affinity with the idea of it being our family home, as it had been our dream to live near to the coast in Queensland. When we found a buyer for the house in Alice Springs, extremely quickly, as was the on-going demand for property there, we sold it furnished with the tenants in place. We decided that we would take a break from city life, and not make rash decisions about our home in Ipswich. We would rent it out temporarily, and live in the woods in Millmerran and see how we felt after that. We could still operate parts of the business in Ipswich, which was only a two-hour drive away, and by condensing our work into longer days, we only needed to work two days a week, principally Tuesday and Thursday. This gave us the income we needed, the ability to visit our house, maintain the garden for the new tenants and ultimately give us the time to progress our self-build in the woods.

The renting arrangement despite being through an agent did not work out. By December 2010, as we prepared for the visit to the UK for Samantha's wedding, we had decided we would keep our home in Ipswich, and live between the two properties, achieving the best of both worlds. There is always an answer; you just have to take a step back sometimes, to reveal it.

Chapter 14
The Good Life

So here we were on our next adventure. A man, a woman, a teenage girl, two dogs, a caravan and a trailer, setting up home in the woods. We had 20 acres of undulating woodland, made up of hard and softwood trees. It was unfenced, with no immediate neighbours other than the incumbent wildlife. This was our little piece of rural paradise hidden from everyone, a blank canvas to create whatever we wanted.

Living the 'good life', from our perspective, and on a practical level, meant aiming to live a simpler existence. In order to fulfil another of our bucket list items, we wanted to pursue a version of 'The Good Life,' inspired by the 1970's UK sitcom, of the same name. 'The Good Life,' for those unfamiliar with its television origins, focused on a suburban couple, Tom and Barbara Good, played by Felicity Kendall and Richard Briers. They opted out of traditional suburban life when Tom reached his fortieth birthday, and decided to quit his conformist office job, as a draughtsman. They embarked on a mission to achieve a simple, yet self-sustainable lifestyle, while still living in the suburbs. To achieve this they changed their conventional gardens into allotments, growing fruit and vegetables for them to eat and with which to barter. In addition they acquired livestock, including chickens, pigs, and a goat, much to their neighbour's disgust.

Over the years in the UK, in the various places that we had lived, we had dabbled with growing vegetables and keeping chickens, in addition to managing a large family, and working full time. However, we had never really considered it in the context of being, in some small way, self-sufficient; it was more of a hobby. This time, we were in pursuit of a healthier and more self-sufficient lifestyle, albeit on a much smaller scale than the television show. We established three large vegetable patches, filling them with plants transplanted from our garden in Ipswich, which gave us a head start. The largest patch, furthest from our base camp, was known as, 'Sarah's secret garden'. I would disappear down there towards the end of the day, light a small fire to keep the mosquitoes away, and sit with my thoughts, my journal and my vegetables.

In addition, Nigel built a chicken hut and enclosure, made from Jaime's old white laminate wardrobe. Well, it was too big to go in the caravan. We bought our first batch of point-of-lay hens in Millmerran, in eager anticipation of them producing eggs for our daily needs. Therefore, it caused great excitement when our chickens produced their first egg. Jaime, who was in charge of egg collection, made a special box for our eggs to be collected and stored in. As usual, Nigel who loves his food was impatient for more. After the initial egg was produced, Jaime continued to collect them at the unhurried rate of one per day, from five chickens!

Patience is a virtue, and as Nigel has very little: distraction with other tasks was the way forward. He constructed dog kennels and a large, secure enclosure for Dave and Buster. Living in the woods with dangerous snakes, which were a big threat to our dogs, the fencing had to be of specific dimensions to prevent unwanted, slithering intruders. Nigel also extended the awning to our caravan, to help protect us from the intensity of the sun by day and to give a larger working area for cooking and relaxing in the evening.

Growing the produce that you need to eat, and keeping chickens for eggs I found to be totally fulfilling. Even though it is hard work, particularly in the intense heat, and with no easy access to a water supply, it did not feel like work, per se. We had to take a huge water tank, on the back of the trailer, to the local borehole, on a regular basis to collect the water we needed for our animals, and to make our vegetables flourish. We collected our drinking water, in large containers, from the town tap, whenever we went to collect groceries, etc.

After acquiring a further caravan from a local woman, our accommodation now consisted of two old caravans, one for Jaime, and one for us; because parents, as well as teenagers, need their own space. Our gas-powered, outdoor kitchen was attached to our caravan by a bench top, and we had a generator, with electric hook ups to the caravans, for use of the fans, laptop and television in the evening, rationed to conserve fuel, as it was a fifty km round trip if we ran out. Managing our laundry in the woods, initially, involved a weekly drive to the nearby country town of Pittsworth, where there was a laundrette, and a supermarket. We would later progress to a second-hand, twin tub washing machine, which looked quite a spectacle on washday in the woods. Nigel would fill it by hand, with several buckets of bore water from the tank; he would then transfer the washing from the washer to the spinner, before line drying it, in the intense Queensland sunshine: no tumble dryer need here. He is a very handy man to have as your husband.

In addition to this, we continued the work of clearing the site to build our own home, albeit in kit form. This again, was a tremendous physical challenge, but a once in-a-lifetime adventure. Our first thoughts of pursuing this particular adventure had come in 2009, after a traumatic year for Nigel. The woods had been a retreat for Nigel in the months immediately after Sheila's passing, providing him with time and space for meditation, reflection, and a coping mechanism to help him carry on. After his return to Alice Springs, we thought on many occasions, about how and when we would be able to afford the time and the money to advance this project. However, when no clear direction was found, we decided that visiting as campers would suffice and we could enjoy the space, and the freedom, whenever we needed it. As I had already experienced the death of my mother, before I met Nigel, for me this was the second time in my lifetime that the realisation hit me that 'life is short.' Far too often, we take the time we have for granted. We expect that we will live a long life, and that we will work, retire and fulfil our long-held dreams and ambitions, after having a career and a family.

Initially, we thought that we would like to build a log cabin, somewhere in the twenty acres, for weekends away and holidays, and that we would be able to make it available to family that visited from overseas. A very vague dream for the future, but vague is good in my world. It gives you the opportunity for vision, change and impulsive behaviour to be expressed. However, when life is brought into perspective by bereavement, you have to question why you wait to pursue your dreams and ambitions. I think it is for this reason: that we felt unsettled in Ipswich, even though we had realised our dream of renovating a house in Queensland, turning it into a family home. Now, after moving to spend time living in the woods in 2010, to take stock of our position again, we had discovered a way of life that gave us our own version of 'the good life'.

Another of our inspirations for designing our woodland retreat was Kevin McCloud, from the UK TV program 'Grand Designs.' We are not architects, and although I enjoy sketching, I am no Picasso. However, we had watched in awe at the transformations and risks which people take to achieve their dream homes. We aspired, on a small scale, to achieve this one day ourselves. However, the mantra of, 'bizarrely they are doing the work by hand, by themselves, and with no clear budget or timeframe,' rang through our ears, on many occasions, over the coming months. Any time that we were hard at work in the woods, at the same time discussing our next objective, one of us would randomly quote those words, and we would laugh together at our little in-house joke. This mantra and our in-house humour are still in use today on our current adventure. Jaime was consistently very positive about the experience. She eagerly embraced life in a small, country town school during our time there. She obviously has some of my positive genes, or as some would say 'her mother's madness'.

Clearing the trees for the construction of our log cabin.

The Queensland climate determined that we would find ourselves being challenged and tested by Mother Nature. Although Queensland is known as the 'Sunshine State', it has its fair share of rain. When you live in the woods, in what most people would consider temporary accommodation, i.e. caravans, when the rain comes, it comes hard, fast and without mercy. We tirelessly struggled to keep it from pooling in the roof awning, and as there was no water supply in the woods, we aimed to collect as much as possible for our vegetable production. Therefore, our site on rainy days, and nights, was an arrangement of water containers in various shapes and sizes. The art of keeping them empty, and transporting the water to the tank, was a spectacle at times. Nigel had a long, green waterproof coat, almost to ankle length, and this, teamed up with his Australian leather, wide brimmed hat made him look like, 'Dr Who, on vacation down-under.'

The tough, practical elements of living in the woods fell to Nigel. Even though I am a physically strong woman, and could do a lot to help him, he organised construction of the temporary and permanent structures. The composting toilet, solar shower room, the digging of the dam, with the dingo digger, and the safety of the site from snakes and spiders, etc. were a few of his successful ventures.

We decided to look for some local work to supplement our income; we had our work in Ipswich, two days a week, and did not want to increase that. The idea was to have a bit more money to kick-start the work in the woods, and get the concrete house slab laid. Finding work in rural Australia is not easy, and we decided it was best if I worked part time at the Millmerran Retirement Home: nurses are hardly ever unemployed, especially when there is an aged care facility nearby.

A teenager living in the woods –
electricity for 1 hour a day, did she hate us?

Jaime started school at Millmerran High School soon after we moved to the woods. She was now fully convalesced from her surgery. The wound was healed, and she was back to her usual, active self. There was a school bus service for the 'children of the woods'. Whenever I heard this phrase used by locals, it would make me think of a Stephen King horror movie. I worried, more than was healthy, about her cycling to the bus stop, and standing in remote rural Australia at the side of the main road that heads to Toowoomba. Thoughts of horror movies like, 'Wolf Creek', plagued me until Nigel told me to "toughen up, and saw some wood".

We were not always totally alone in the woods, apart from the wildlife; we also had a surreal experience when one night a white Persian cat strolled into our campsite to eat the remains of the dog biscuits. Where would a cat like that come from? Had new neighbours moved into our secluded area? Feeling sorry for the cat, which we surmised must have been dumped in the woods, we provided food and water. A ginger Tomcat joined the Persian the following night. They did not appear to be friends and the ruckus they made caused Nigel to have to get up during the night to investigate, thinking maybe snakes had entered the camp and were attacking the cats.

As the days went by the cats became more at home with us, much to the disgust of our boys and our chickens. Then one day, as Jaime was on her mobile phone in her tree house and I was collecting wood for fence making, we heard cat meowing from behind a fallen tree. As we watched from a distance, we noticed a black cat, which we had not seen before. However, the cat meowing was still coming from the fallen tree and not from the black cat. Approaching quietly it soon became apparent that a litter of kittens had been born there and the black cat was protecting them. We did not touch or go near them, as we really did not want to encourage any more cats into the camp. However, the kittens had other ideas. One evening as we sat enjoying a cold beer, sitting outside our motor home, Nigel thought he saw something in the wheel arch. It was twilight and not easy to see so we did not pursue it. Later that evening, we were inside the motor home relaxing, about to watch a DVD, when meowing could be heard, albeit very faintly. Nigel lifted the floor hatch that exposed the engine, and there was a tiny, black kitten looking very frightened. It hid in the crevices of the engine parts, which we could not access, so we had to leave it. Over the coming days, the kitten would routinely be heard, or briefly glimpsed in or around the motor home. A few days passed, and we noticed that the food that we left out was not being eaten, until eventually it was not touched at all. The cats had gone, just as quickly and stealthily as they had arrived.

Nigel celebrated his birthday in the woods, and on the Friday before, during our regular laundry outing to Pittsworth, I took him to a small coffee shop. This was more than just having a coffee; it was a chance to feel 'normal' for half an hour. Sitting on soft, brown, leather sofas, instead of camp chairs, with the aroma of freshly made coffee wafting around, intermingling with the smell of baking croissants and bread, was reminiscent of being on holiday in France. What is this feeling of 'normal?' I have often struggled with this concept, as I do not believe that I have ever neatly fitted into the 'normal' criteria. However, today's normal was about sitting in a comfortable chair, drinking a cappuccino, and making chitchat with my wonderful husband. We had not done this for longer than is healthy, due to our self-induced, hectic lifestyle, and continuous saving and care with our finances.

For his birthday the following day, we decided to attend the

Millmerran annual sheep-racing event. I know, 'what were we thinking?' The plan was afterwards to have a lovely, home-cooked meal of fresh salmon and home-grown vegetables, accompanied by a nice bottle of wine and some well-deserved relaxation for Nigel. Sheep racing was another first for us, and we were not sure that we should condone this sport by attending, but our curiosity got the better of us. It was quite a surreal experience. We arrived at the showground and wandered in, looking for the advertised pre-racing entertainment and fun fair. All of the above was non-existent, save for a small bouncy castle for young children, and some older children taking turns in sumo wrestling suits, writhing around in the dirt, none of which was Jaime's idea of fun. Suddenly she looked very grown up.

Unable to entertain Jaime with the funfair, we thought we would try the food tent and experience rural Queensland cuisine. However, as we were vegetarian at that time, the only sustenance available to us was a cone of hot chips, which did not live up to their description. They were hardly warm, and with no salt or vinegar available, they were, 'very ordinary' as they say, in Australia. We decided lunch could wait until after the racing, when we would head to the café in the town. We found ourselves some good seats, up in the pavilion-seating stand overlooking the track. I should explain now that the show ground resembles, and I later discovered doubles, as the livestock market.

Without intending to sound like a snob again, some people in attendance looked like stereotypical Australians, from television comic sketches. The women, wearing too much makeup for the Queensland sun, heat and humidity, and the men, in their cowboy hats and boots, some wearing the obligatory wife beater vest with a food and beer stained front, which is unattractive even on a well-toned body.

Eventually, ten sheep lined up at the start, each with an individual-named teddy bear strapped to their backs, as riders. As the starter gun went off the sheep left the gates, slowly! One decided to turn back towards the start, while most decided to stand still after a few steps forward, until three men got behind them to 'encourage' them on. Eventually, they were all running, and literally following each other, like sheep. Obviously, the one who was in front at the start was the winner, because all the others did was to follow, with no attempt to overtake. The winner was, 'Helen's Heels'. In retrospect, it was not very humane, and not entertaining, so we left after the first race. Even though I am a born and bred country girl from Suffolk, and I have been to many country shows and fairs which have animal sports, the way the sheep were poked and prodded for entertainment left a lot to be desired. It is 'official': we are now residents in a rural country town, having attended our first community event.

In October, with news that we were getting a long-stay visitor, we decided that more accommodation was required. After seeing a motor home for sale at the side of the road, at another woods property, we decided that this uncared-for 1978 Toyota coaster motor home conversion would be an ideal project for us. We named her 'Itchy feet' because she would be our escape vehicle when we needed a change of scenery. We would use it as extra living space initially, while working on it to make it roadworthy for future travelling and exploring around Australia. It was not much to look at on the outside, needing some filling and a paint job, but the inside had everything we needed. There was a double bed, separate kitchenette with gas fridge, oven and hob and, the best thing of all, a small portable toilet with a curtain surrounding it. What a luxury. An indoor toilet for night time usage meant no more battling to avoid huntsman spiders and snakes by torch light in the darkness of the woods.

Phillip had decided to come out on an ETA, (Electronic Travel Authority, or tourist visa), to help with the clearing and construction in the woods. This was a great opportunity for Nigel and Phillip to spend some quality time together. They have many similar traits, and watching them complete boxing training exercise routines in the intense Queensland humidity and sunshine, was quite a spectacle: a perfect scene of father and son bonding. Life in the woods was hard, but rewarding in unusual ways, and because of this, I think it was a great experience for him, as he found out first-hand what interests his dad and what he really enjoys. Finding out that they shared similar interests was a bonus, and as it turned out Phillip shared Nigel's passion for the security industry. After returning to the UK with us in December, for the wedding, he went on to obtain his security license in the UK.

After a couple of months, we started to encounter issues with the rental of our house in Ipswich. We decided that we would not pursue that any further, and that having made a lovely family home, we had the perfect opportunity of having two properties, which we could live between. This would give us the best of both worlds, city and country living. We decided that working out the logistics of that arrangement could wait until we got back from the UK in January, after Samantha's wedding. We remained positive that our Australian adventure in Queensland, would continue and we were excited to establish our new five-year plan, in consultation with the children, during our visit to the UK when they would all at last be together with us in the same place, at the same time.

Chapter 15
Losing it all to flood water

"If I am what I have, and if I lose what I have, who then am I?"
Erich Fromm.

I think I have always believed in fate, and the ideology that
'everything happens for a reason'. However, trying to rationalise the
'reason' for the events during and after January 2011 caused me to
struggle with this concept, and if there is a 'reason,' it had better be a
good one.

Samantha was due to get married in Looe, Cornwall, UK on 11th
January 2011. We decided to surprise her by arranging earlier than
planned flights to the UK, so that we would arrive on her doorstep on
Christmas Day. I do not know why we thought travelling so close to
Christmas would be good idea. I think we, or I, became carried away
with the romantic, chick lit notions of it all. My perfect vision was of
Samantha, whose family lived on the other side of the world,
answering the door on Christmas morning to find them standing there,
just when she thought she would spend another Christmas missing
them, etc. Well, I suppose I watch too many girlie films and read too
many romantic fiction novels.

The journey got off to a shaky start when we almost missed our
connecting flight in Sydney. Our flight from Brisbane to Sydney was
delayed by a thunderstorm. When we finally arrived in Sydney, we
had to make a frenzied run from the domestic arrivals terminal to the
international departure terminal. With Nigel and Phillip in lead
positions, and Jaime and I bringing up the rear, we were determined
that we would catch our Malaysia airlines flight to London Heathrow,
if we just kept running. At the time, we thought how lucky we were
that we did not have to collect our luggage after the Brisbane domestic
flight, or we surely would not have made it to international departures
on time. Thank goodness for being able to check the luggage in for the
whole journey from Brisbane.

With an exhausted sigh of relief, we took our seats, the last people onto the plane. It was not our imagination; everybody was looking at us with that impatient look of, 'we are all waiting for you'. Hot and sweaty, we were targeted by disapproving stares as we struggled to put our hand luggage into the overhead lockers and take our seats. This was to the obvious annoyance of a young couple who thought their luck was in, with four empty seats that they could have spread out on for a comfortable sleep during the long flight, if we had not made it in time. However, as far as we were concerned the main thing was it was all OK: we had made the flight. The flights were long, and after watching multiple inflight movies and eating an enormous amount of meals provided, after a quick stop in Kuala Lumpur, we eventually arrived at Heathrow on time. It was Christmas Day and yes, it was snowing; the iconic white Christmas. The temperature was -2 °C at six o'clock in the morning, and coming from peak summertime in Australia, we were unsuitably dressed in tee shirts, cotton trousers and thongs (flip-flops) on our feet.

As we stood at the baggage reclaim area the realisation soon dawned that we had not been as lucky with our luggage, as we had first thought. Sadly, our luggage had not completed the journey with us. This was quickly apparent as the other passengers left and the dizzying conveyor belt circled in front of us, empty apart from some stray remnants of luggage tags and a broken pushchair that no-one claimed. Nigel and I looked at each other: it was like that scene from 'Home alone', when they realise that Kevin is missing. The sense of realisation, denial and then horror at the implications of what this meant hit us. This was not mere holiday luggage that had failed to arrive: it was items of Samantha's wedding ensemble and suitable winter clothing, which we desperately needed at this particular moment, as we stood shivering at the lost baggage desk completing numerous forms. All of our wedding outfits, gifts, paperwork, etc., were missing in action.

Anyway, now that the reality of these travel plans was plain to see, instead of thinking 'I can't wait to see the look on her face', I now thought 'what a nightmare'. Nigel, in his own forthright style, reminded me that I was being over-dramatic, and in hindsight, it was not that bad, but at the time I really did not need any hassle on top of jet lag! At the lost baggage desk, they soon discovered our luggage was still in Brisbane. Therefore, we were given the princely sum of forty-five pounds each, as compensation for the inconvenience. Forty-five pounds - did they have any idea what the consequences would be if our bags did not arrive? Anyway, we were told that our bags would be delivered in the next two days. Bearing in mind it was now Christmas Day, the likely hood of the next two-day deadline being met was extremely unlikely. However, the wedding was not until 11th January so there was no need to panic, just yet!

Walking through customs choosing the 'nothing to declare' exit, when the 'nothing to wear' exit would have been more appropriate, we must have looked very suspicious in our limited casual clothing and sunglasses. My imagination got the better of me and I had visions of being called to one side and strip-searched, as we had no bags and few clothes to conceal anything. However, we were not stopped and we proceeded to the courtesy bus, which would take us to the car hire pick up point. Everyone around us was wearing thick coats, boots and scarves, while we tiptoed through the snow and ice, shaking from head to foot. I could feel everybody looking at us, but what could we do: they don't sell winter clothes in the duty-free shop. Luckily the car hire documents were in Nigel's hand luggage, and so once the car keys were obtained and we were inside the car, the heater was put on full blast. It remained on for the entire journey.

We drove cautiously through some treacherous conditions and finally arrived in Liskeard just after midday. Our plan was simple: I would call Samantha on her mobile phone, at the same time as Nigel would go and ring the doorbell, she would say hang on there's someone at the door and I would wait on the phone for the 'surprise!' Pretty much that is exactly how our little surprise panned out. Lots of hugs, tears, and laughter, especially at us standing in snow and ice wear summer clothes. Jaime and I quickly took advantage of Samantha's wardrobe and its contents.

Now this was Christmas as I remembered it. Christmas day television on in the background, dinner being cooked with anybody willing to help doing so, and Jaime eager to open a present, any present, even if it was not for her. We made telephone calls to the other children and our schedule of visits and pick up, etc. was made. We were happy; we were going to see all of the children over this Christmas and New Year period. It felt awesome, and the memories of the last two Christmases were now deeply buried.

The Christmas and New Year period with all of our children, in the lead up to the wedding, was amazing, having not seen them altogether for such a long time. As a big family group, we took over two, eight-berth caravans at the holiday resort in Looe where Samantha was working. The day after New Year, we moved to a holiday house on the sea-front with four bedrooms and plenty of space for the wedding day preparations.

On the days leading up to the wedding we had watched on Sky news the horrific images and tragic news footage of the inland tsunami that washed through the country town of Toowoomba. It was approximately an hour's drive in each direction from our woodland in Millmerran and our house in Ipswich. We wondered about people we knew from Millmerran who worked there or visited regularly to see family and friends. As the tsunami was confined to the flood plains, we were just grateful that our properties were not near enough to be impacted.

In the early hours of the morning, 11th January 2011, we were awake after having missed calls on both of our mobile phones. They were numbers we didn't recognise so we assumed maybe they were the travel insurance people checking that our luggage had arrived, which it had, four days after our arrival, thank goodness. Drinking tea and going over the schedule for the day's events, we were now watching the Brisbane floods on Sky news. A sense of horror mixed with disbelief surged through us as we watched images of cars floating like boats through streets we had driven down. People were crying and desperately trying to check on the safety and whereabouts of family members. Alarm bells started to ring in our heads and panic ensued. Working out that the missed calls were from somewhere with a Brisbane telephone number, our immediate concern was then for Dave and Buster who were in kennels there. A frantic phone call reassured us that they were unaffected and that all was well, they kennel staff told us that John had called them from Tasmania after watching the footage on the national news. Next, we called to check on the car, which was at the Brisbane airport parking. A call them to confirmed that all cars were safe and unaffected. We felt somewhat reassured, but still anxious. However, as it stood as far as we knew, all was well in Ipswich, although we felt a deep sadness for the people we were watching on television struggling to retrieve their precious personal possessions from the dirty floodwater. While we had been frantically making calls, another caller was trying to get through to us. This call was not good news. A friend called to say Jacaranda Street in Ipswich had been, in parts, affected by floodwater, and that our property had been 'breached,' but that she could not tell us more than that at this stage as the area was cordoned off.

What does that even mean, 'breached'? We were told it would be at least forty-eight hours before the State Emergency Service (SES) crews would let homeowners in to assess the damage, and so we decided, as there really was nothing we could do, that it would be fine. Positive as ever, I convinced myself that they probably meant the garden had been breached. Our house was on a corner plot and on a hill, nowhere near the River Bremer that had apparently burst its banks, so there was no way the house could have been 'breached.' No dramas, as they say in Australia. We would continue with the wedding day and we could deal with whatever had happened when we got home. We had plans for the entertaining area in the garden anyway, so this would be good excuse to bring these plans forward. We could not share our concerns or worries with anyone, except each other, not on Samantha's wedding day.

Wedding Day celebrations

The wedding day was spectacular. Samantha looked like a princess and our girls, Clair, Molly and Jaime were beautiful bridesmaids. Our sons, Phillip and Robert looked like proper gents in their smart suits. We felt so proud; it was such a special day with so many close, personal moments between mother and daughter, and stepfather and stepdaughter. Samantha's biological father had refused to attend her wedding, as he had not been given the role of walking her down the aisle. Bearing in mind their quite distant relationship, I think she made the right decision, but it was still disappointing for her that he did not attend.

Sarah Jane the proud mother of the beautiful bride Samantha

Even though it was January, the sun shone. There was still snow in places and the roads were icy. This was a slight problem for the ladies of the wedding party. In stiletto heels, trying to walk downhill on ice was impossible. Therefore, we had to take off our shoes and change into our trainers. Holding onto our shoes and the stone walls we made our way cautiously to the waiting wedding cars. This spectacle on a cold winter's morning was highly amusing to the many onlookers that gathered in the small streets of Looe. For anyone who knows the small seaside town of Looe, the lanes are small, steep and winding. Not all lanes are accessible by a full size car, as they were originally built for carts to convey fish from the harbour; therefore walking was the only option. Nigel said afterwards that it was a very special moment, walking Samantha down the steep lane to the car, just the two of them, arm in arm. They have a very close bond, which was clear for all to see that day. Despite the nerves of being in the spotlight, they both smiled all the way down the aisle, with an occasional caring glance to each other to make sure everything was OK. A local singer, who was a close friend of Samantha, was singing 'Ave Maria'. It was truly beautiful, and the sound track accompanied the CD of photographs afterwards. I was crying, as most mums do at this point in the proceedings. My first born, my little girl who was already a woman was now going into the care of someone else. A hard concept when your gut tells you something is not right, but you have nothing to base that instinct on.

At the wedding reception our family and friends, some of whom we had not seen for a few years, were all together and most importantly, all of our children were together in the same room, dancing, laughing and having fun. As a mum, I was so happy and proud of our big family. As I hugged Doug as they left for their honeymoon night at a local hotel, I told him to take care of my little girl. He said he would, and I believed him.

A few days later, when all the tearful good byes to the children had been said, we started our long journey home to Australia. As we started the arduous, thirty-six hour flight schedule, which would enforce sleep deprivation, all we could think about was what we would find when we got back. As the final flight landed in Brisbane, a sense of impending doom filled my thoughts. I do not know why, suddenly, when I had felt positive up to this point about the whole situation since we had received the telephone call. I think it was the reality of landing and going to see for ourselves what 'breached' meant.

We collected our car, and drove to collect Dave and Buster from the kennels which was in one of the nearby suburbs. As we headed home to Ipswich to start a new year, we had no idea what an impact the flood would have on the rest of our time in Australia. The drive from Brisbane to Ipswich is usually only forty minutes, but parts of the journey were like driving through news footage of a disaster zone. Rightly so, because this was a huge natural disaster. The severity varied from area to area, some places were almost unaffected whereas others displayed the remains of flood invasion. Piles of debris from local businesses and homes had been shovelled to the side of the road, ready for the council to collect and dispose of. Despite the intensity of the damage, as we drove past we could make out the remains of pictures, photographs, items of furniture, the remains of people's lives reduced to a pile of waterlogged debris. It was heart breaking.

'Breached' was the word that had been used to describe the condition of our property. What this actually meant was 'submerged up to the level of the roof'. Our home, a high set Queenslander set on a corner plot on a hill, made it hard to imagine or visualize what the house and garden would have looked like under water. The evidence of the flood was apparent immediately, with food packaging on our roof and the silt embedded tidemark around the house where the water had settled just under the facia boards. It was like a dirty scum ring left in the bath after a teenaged boy had used it. The windows, fly screens and doors were either missing or hanging off their hinges from where the exiting water pressure had forced them open. The steep concrete driveway was thick with mud and silt, and the SES 'Danger Do Not Enter' tape surrounded the house. A large crack in the concrete and brickwork on the left side of the building indicated why it was not safe to enter. Against my advice, Nigel carefully made his way up the driveway and walked around to the back of the house, as Jaime and I remained in the car. He found remnants of dog bowls and bedding squashed against the wire fence by the force of the water. Many pieces of broken kitchen units, wood, metal and items of unknown origin littered the ground. He would not tell me in detail what else he saw and I know why. He did not want me to have the image of things that were personal to us, from the house that we renovated into a home, destroyed in such a callous way by Mother Nature.

The entertaining area was thick with mud, and as Nigel carefully made his way back to the car, the look of shock, sadness and disbelief was obvious. We sat in silence in the car, looking down the street that was now unrecognisable: this felt surreal. The normally bustling street was quiet and empty, with just piles of debris to acknowledge what had happened there in our absence. In a state of disbelief, but thinking on our feet, we decided to head to the caravans and the motor home in

Millmerran woods where we at least had somewhere to go. Many people were at the mercy of the rescue centres set up by the Red Cross and Salvation Army. We did not want to take advantage of the resources they made available when others more in need had nowhere else to go. It was mid-summer, the temperatures were in the high thirties, so living exposed to the heat and humidity would be intense, but we had a good set up there and we knew we could manage.

The drive back to the woods was horrific in its own way, due to not only our shocked state of mind, but also the sights we saw on the way. The large expanse of fields, which should have been filled with crops, had been flattened beyond recognition. Australian farmers are sadly used to having crops destroyed by bushfires and drought. They support each other and their communities to rebuild and restart their businesses, but this was different. This was floods and it was not just the farmers affected, it was the whole community. Lives had been lost, including a teenaged boy swept away from the roof of a car in Toowoomba because he made the rescuers take his mum and younger brother first. How do people recover from this type of disaster? It was a very humbling experience and put the worries that we may have had into perspective.

As we approached Toowoomba, we feared for what we might see. Again, the tidemarks on the buildings told the tale of destruction. We could not bear to stop; we did not want to see. Only an hour away from Millmerran, we now had to consider if our caravan and motor home had been affected. How widespread had the forces of nature been? Did we have anything left? Fortunately the only damage to our caravans was from sand that had blown or been washed through the camp, nothing that could not be cleaned up or moved. It did make me cry to see that the rain from the storm that had accompanied the Toowoomba tsunami, had leaked into our storage area where some of our personal effects were stored. Nigel quickly reminded me that there were many much worse off than us. What mattered now was that we had shelter, we were safe and we were together. So there it was, that at a time of indecision prior to leaving for the wedding, things had happened to take some of the decision-making out of our hands. From considering

119

renting, selling and living between the two properties we would now lose them both. The bank, in approximately nine months' time would repossess them, because the mortgage on Jacaranda Street was secured on the woodland in Millmerran, as it was an asset. The process would be slow, painful, frustrating, and bureaucratic, but we were only one family out of many who would suffer at the hands of Mother Nature. We were lucky, if anyone can be considered lucky in these circumstances: we lost property and material goods, but there were people who lost members of their family, suffered miscarriages and stillbirths and/or lost their pets.

During the two weeks that followed, I think we were in shock, or at least I was. Disbelief, shock, anger, frustration, despair, the list could be endless, and ultimately useless. The range of emotions and feelings are without meaning, when you feel as if you have lost everything you have worked so hard to achieve. It was as if it was not happening to us, that we were spectators watching a television reality show. However, time and banks wait for no-one to recover from shock, and so we had to start to try to salvage the remains of our life and decide what to do, and where to go next.

Chapter 16
Relocation: Queensland to Tasmania

Decision made, it's time to swap Queensland for Tasmania. The relocation begins.

It is time to contend with the flood aftermath. The king-tide in Brisbane, and the coincidental opening of the Wivenhoe Dam, near Toowoomba, changed our lives. Good times, hard times, highs and lows, everyone experiences them. The trick is to find a way through the maze of tangled webs with which we weave our lives together. The ability to overcome the challenges in our lives makes us stronger and better people. When each day is a struggle, and the light of hope that we seek is not a bright beacon, but an oxygen-starved flame burning away, self-doubt enters. The sense of anxiety, nervousness, pressure and helplessness become normal. These feelings lift temporarily when interrupted by the strength and kindness of the people who love and care for you. The emotional turmoil experienced is sometimes hard to understand for the people trying to offer support, and comfort. Frustration and helplessness ensues.

The restoration of 'life' as it existed, not the restoration of the material items, is the ultimate 'win–win' situation, and to achieve this we ended up with two choices.

One – fight on.

Two – concede defeat.

We did not consider the second choice, so finding the strength to fight on became the overriding focus to restore life to a semblance of normality. Even with the positive approach of fighting on, the realisation soon emerged that to some extent the result meant a degree of defeat. The defeat characterised by the end of our Queensland adventure, at least for the time being. In the coming months, we would lose our woodland in Millmerran, which was security for the purchase of our flooded house in Ipswich. Therefore, with little incentive to complete any further work or invest any more money into the project, reality dawned. The immense sadness that this brought to us is hard to verbalise, and still brings tears to my eyes to think, or even write about it. This unassuming piece of woodland held so many special memories for Nigel. Together, we had found peace and serenity: our secret hideaway, where we could tell our secrets to our trees and the wildlife, who shared it with us. We had the ability to laugh, cry, shout or do whatever we wanted; unobserved, with no one to judge us and with complete freedom.

There were only two possibilities. The first, to return to the UK: this was not a realistic consideration, with all of the bureaucracy to sort out. The second was to relocate to Tasmania, to live with my father-in-law, John. In the here and now of those first few days, we knew our choices were limited. Our house in Ipswich was unfit to enter, let alone live in; and now, no prospect of being able to finance our self-build or retain ownership of our woodland. Relocation to Tasmania revealed itself as the only sensible option for us to start again.

We had lengthy discussions with John over the next few days and he decided he would fly to Queensland and help us to organise for the interstate move. Within four days, Nigel picked John up at Brisbane airport. His visit also had another special reason behind it; he had seen photographs of our woodland project, but wanted to see it for real. He knew how much retreating there had helped Nigel after Sheila died, and he wanted to see this place which Nigel held so dear. John experienced the intense, unforgiving heat and humidity of outback Queensland from the moment he arrived. We would get up early in the morning, before the sun rose causing the extreme temperatures to sap our strength, giving us the opportunity to perform physical tasks. In the afternoons, we would follow the areas of shade around the edge of our clearing for some respite. On a few occasions, we succumbed and resorted to putting our solitary air conditioner unit on, just for an hour, to cool our core temperatures. Dehydration presented a big risk, as we worked to disassemble structures, etc. However, a nice cold beer in the late afternoon became a well-deserved treat. However, you had to drink plenty of water in-between otherwise you suffered the consequences.

I am not a materialistic person, never have been. The loss of assets, personal effects, and property, whatever you want to call it, did not devastated me as much as the loss of our dreams; our vision. Our Australian dream, swept away with the tide. For the first time since we had arrived in Australia, I had a sense of loss and vulnerability. The concept of 'losing your roots' is a difficult thing to come to terms with, but despite this we would not consider for a single moment returning to the UK. We were still in Australia, safe, healthy, and we would continue our Australian adventure. Therefore, with our dreams squashed we accepted the reality of our circumstances and set about finding a new focus and direction. We would not wallow in self-pity or just curl up and die. You cannot die from this anyway, so life has to go on. We set about trying to organise ourselves for an interstate move, once again. As fond as we are of a road trip this one would be a corker. However, before we got to that stage we had to organise our belongings in the woods.

As John's visit ended, he filled his suitcase with photographs and special items that we did not want to risk on the road trip. We continued packing up our belongings in the woods, until another unwelcome interruption occurred. At a time when I did not want to deliberate anymore about anything stressful, I received an appointment in Brisbane to attend a psychological assessment. It was part of the personal injury proceedings following the road rage car accident, back in April 2010, which had resulted in my PTSD. Why did this have to happen now? After telephone calls to the legal team handling my case, it appeared there was no option but to attend. As we were due to relocate, they did at least agree to bring the appointment forward so that I would not have to travel back from Tasmania. Therefore, three days later we set off to Brisbane.

A harrowing four-hour car journey each way for anyone has its own pressures. However, for someone already in a state of high anxiety, as our interstate move approached, combined with a two-hour appointment, the effects were traumatising. The psychological assessment consisted of what resembled an interrogation in a faceless room of a private clinic. At first the questions were, I suppose, geared to filter out people who may exaggerate their symptoms and incapacity in the hope of a higher compensation payment. At this moment in time, I was not interested, and so my obvious honesty put me through to the next stage. The psychiatrist then questioned me about local and national events.

"Tell me about a story in the news, other than the floods."

I was numb; my brain seized like a rusty bolt. No words entered my mouth as I attempted to speak; I must have looked like an idiot. It was silent for what seemed like hours, but in reality, were only minutes. I thought we might progress to some easier questions now, but then he started questioning me about my anxiety levels on the four-hour car journey to the appointment. At this point, I lost control, crying with no-one, other than this hard faced man across the desk from me, to comfort me. Therefore, I just cried. He left the room and I tried to compose myself. When he returned, he said it might help to document my thoughts. This I considered was a bad move on his part. I enjoy writing and he gave me the opportunity to give him the full extent of my frustration of this ordeal. The pages of his A4 lined writing pad filled with my inner most thoughts as he sat watching me. My tears continued falling on the paper, smudging the ink. Then, just as they had started, my tears stopped. I looked up, and he was writing. I knew he was writing about me, so I just stared at him. He rubbed his balding head and asked me to go to the waiting area. I knew he now needed reading time. I sat there for forty-five minutes before he called me in again.

"It is obvious that you are very upset today, and I think we have all we need for now", he said, getting to his feet and gesturing towards the door.

The receptionist gave me an attendance form to sign and then I was free to leave. I almost ran out of the building. I sent a text to Nigel to come and pick me up and he arrived within a few minutes. In the busy CBD, he could not stop to hug me, but I knew I was safe now with him. On the four-hour journey, back the mood was sombre; I did not want to talk about what happened.

The day before we left the woods a copy of the psychological assessment arrived in the post. I did not want to read it, so Nigel did.

After a few minutes, he said, "I don't think this is the right report, it's not about you".

Intrigued, I asked, "Why?"

"Well, it says here that you presented as a woman dressed for your age, in a skirt and blouse. I thought you wore jeans and tee-shirt that day, you don't wear skirts in the woods". He continued reading and occasionally looked up at me. There were fifteen pages and when he reached the end he said, "OK, he says you're depressed and angry".

'Depressed and angry,' is that the best he could do. The letter that accompanied the report said no further assessments would be required, that was all I needed to know. It would be six months before I read that report in detail.

Over the next two weeks, we found it hard to look forward. Normally being able to find the positive in any situation, I struggled to find something good that could come out of our current circumstances. Not for the first time in our relationship, Nigel kick-started me back into positive action. He reminded me that I determined how, and if, I would let uncontrollable events affect me. If I chose to let the circumstances control me then that was my choice.

I went back to my journal feeling a bit sorry for myself, like a child having been told off. I decided to read my journal from other stressful or challenging times, to see if the strategies used then could help me now. I remembered reading about this approach in a self-coaching book. I read about a traumatic episode that occurred when we were living in Alice Springs. With tears in my eyes and somewhat daunted, as the recollection of that episode was more upsetting than my present dilemma, no new answers appeared. However, as I put pen to paper to work out the pros and cons of the current situation a strange thing happened. I was supposed to be writing a list of the pros and cons, but I was unable to think of one single pro, as the list of cons pierced my eyes. Then I had one of those light bulb moments; I have experienced them in the past and they have often moved my life in many and varied directions. Was I looking at this whole situation from the wrong angle? Perhaps the answer was to put myself outside the box and look in on our situation. What would someone looking in on us do or think? I might be able to move the pieces of this jigsaw puzzle, which represents our life, to complete the picture. In addition, in doing so I might reveal a path out of the turmoil, which we were now enduring. Staring at the words that started to appear on the blank page in front of me, a new direction, a new way of thinking developed. I realised that if I took the material factors like the house, the woods, etc. out of the equation, and focused on our emotional and psychological needs, I did have the answers. The tools and life experience to help us move forward were available for me to tap into. My mind-set started to regain some clarity: the process of packing for an interstate move with my loving husband, my teenage daughter and our two 'boys' now became my all-consuming mission.

Therefore, with the chickens, Jaime's guinea pig and my precious vegetable plants distributed between the nursing home and members of the local community, we continued disassembling as many of our structures as possible. We put the wood and corrugated tin into the caravans and motor home, as building supplies are valuable assets in the woods. Although we did not know it at the time, fortunately our motor home, worth less than five thousand dollars, would not be included in any future financial proceedings. The caravans were not worth trying to sell or move; therefore, we planned to leave them. However, our 'Itchy feet,' motor home was different. The money to buy, 'Itchy feet' had come from a small inheritance that Nigel received from his mums estate, and therefore had special significance for him. Although we would have to leave 'her' there for now, as we took our belongings to Tasmania, we would then fly back in two weeks to retrieve her. We would have a small window of opportunity, of two or three weeks, to move and travel back to collect anything else that we valued, before it would be gone.

Road trip from Millmerran Woods, Queensland to Copping, Tasmania

Here we go again: our 4WD and trailer full to overflowing with two adults, a teenage girl, two very noisy dogs and all our worldly possessions. Now not many people can have that as a boast! Thankfully, Nigel is an expert at packing, anything from a car to the weekly food shopping: if there is a space, he will fill it. I should explain that although 'our boys' love to go out for a drive they bark continuously. This becomes frustrating and annoying, because reprimanding them does nothing to quieten them. Therefore, you can imagine how our tolerance would be tested on such a long journey.

Australia has six states and two territories; and on this trip, we would travel through four of the states, Queensland, New South Wales, Victoria and Tasmania. The journey to Tasmania would span over two thousand kilometres of road travel. In addition, it would include an overnight ferry between Port Melbourne, Victoria, and Devonport, North Tasmania. The last leg of the road trip would take us from Devonport to Hobart, South Tasmania.

The first leg of our road trip from Millmerran Woods to Port Melbourne would take two full days of driving, and one overnight stop. This would mean all of us, including the dogs, 'sleeping' in the car. Obviously, the quality of the sleep in the cramped conditions, heat, humidity, flies and with our excited 'boys' in the back would be limited. Nigel did all of the driving because of my PTSD and driving anxiety, for which I was consumed with guilt. Even if I could have driven, he would not have let me. I trust Nigel's driving unreservedly. Despite my acquired personal fears of travelling, I would be sitting in the passenger seat trying to keep myself calm and hide my anxiety from Jaime. Therefore, Nigel put me in charge of refreshments, entertainment, (which meant keeping Nigel awake), and some aspects of navigation, though I prefer not to be involved in navigation as maps confuse me. Nigel's cue for needing my unique form of entertainment

127

when he was getting tired was, "talk to me". Therefore, I did; I talked about 'crap' as he called it and kept him supplied with food and coffee on the go.

Our road trip took longer than most car travellers did on this route, as we needed to make frequent stops for the 'boys' to drink, and then for toilet stops. With no air con in the 4WD due to a collision with a kangaroo that resulted in the breaking of the compressor, keeping cool was a big problem. We also needed to stretch our legs and keep our circulation going after sitting in cramped conditions. Jaime, with very limited space allocated to her on the back seat, had an array of things to keep her entertained, her mobile phone, Nintendo games and various magazines, etc. Despite all of this, she claimed to be 'bored,' continuously.

We stopped for the night in a lay-by on the Newell Highway, near to a place called Parkes, New South Wales. This town has been famously known as the 'Elvis Capital of Australia' since the start of the annual Elvis Festivals in 1993. Held each January as a tourism boost, it once hosted a new world record achievement in 2007 for having the largest number of Elvis impersonators at one event. However, Parkes is also the location of 'The Dish', a huge radio telescope that can be seen for miles. It was made famous in the movie of the same name, which fictionalised the story of 'The Dish,' during the Apollo space program in the late 1960s.

Parkes was originally a gold mining, canvas settlement, called Currajong. It later changed its name to Bushmans in the 1860s and '70s. Known as a 'canvas settlement,' because of the tents erected for the workers to live in, it became one of the most prosperous gold mining towns in Australia. Sir Henry Parkes, the Prime Minister of New South Wales, showed his support for the township by visiting there in the mid 1870s. In honour of his support, the town's name was changed to Parkes, a short time later. As he originated from Coventry, in the UK, the town of Parkes is now twinned with Coventry to honour him.

Anyway, back to Jaime, whose worst fears had now been realised.

All of her electrical and battery operated devices had run out of power. We had no means of recharging them, as the cigarette lighter was in use for the car fridge, cold drinks, and the 'boys' fan in the back. Her teenage boredom and frustration displayed itself in the form of sulking; because of course, we were to blame. As tiredness kicked in, frustration mounted and tempers became frayed.

As the light faded, and refreshed after plenty of food and drink, we walked around the lay-by, taking care not to encounter snakes and spiders in the undergrowth. However, rest beckoned and we all succumbed. We struggled with our regular road trip car game of 'windows up and we fry in the heat or windows down, and we are eaten alive by mosquitoes'. Tensions ran high in our little world that night. Nigel, having longer legs than either Jaime or I struggled the most to get into a comfortable position to sleep. He ended up with his head against the side window in the foetal position, dozing but not sleeping. As the food and other provisions were in my foot well, I assumed a crouched position on the front passenger seat. Jaime meanwhile tossed and turned in her upright sleeping position. However, being a teenager she managed to sleep, God knows how, but we hoped that sleep might improve her mood for the next leg of the journey. In the early hours of the morning, as trucks continued to thunder past on the main highway, we decided to abandon all hope of sleep. If we set off now and made it to Melbourne early, we could find a car park to attempt to sleep again, as we waited for the ferry.

We arrived in Melbourne, hours ahead of our ferry, so we looked for a car park near the sea front to park up. After walking the 'boys' we stretched out on the grassed area in the warm February sun: it felt amazing after the journey endured so far. It is a unique feeling taking a road trip that is not a holiday or a well-planned interstate move. This trip of necessity, planned within a few weeks and unintended, resulted in us leaving mainland Australia. In some respects, we felt as though we were leaving Australia itself, and maybe we were subconsciously.

As our departure time for the eleven-hour ferry trip to Tasmania approached, we drove nearer to the Port. We parked in a lay-by opposite some very expensive looking apartments, much to the obvious disgust of one of the residents. He was collecting his pampered pooch from the mobile dog groomers parked at the entrance to the complex. He looked across at us with loathing. I suppose we did look quite scruffy and dishevelled, in our battered and dusty 4WD with its trailer adorned with items strapped to every available surface. In addition, our two noisy dogs in the back barked at the windows like caged bears. He must have thought we look like gypsy travellers and that we were going to devalue his property by daring to stop there. Anyway, we were too tired to find anywhere else, so we ignored him.

We sat gazing out to sea at the horizon, as the beachfront played host to a boot camp training session for what looked like a local football team. Joggers and cyclists randomly passed along the promenade in front of us, while our jumbled and mixed emotions became numb with fatigue. Tired of thinking and weary from the journey, I'd had enough. I needed to pull myself together; we were a team, and there is no 'I' in team. Therefore, it was vital that we stayed strong, to have any chance at restarting our Australian adventure in Tasmania.

When the ferry terminal gates opened, we joined the queue. The process of loading the array of trucks, cars, caravans and motorbikes began, all very efficiently. With dogs to transport, we needed to go to a special cargo area with on-board kennels, giving the 'boys' access to water during the trip. Nigel settled them in, with their own bedding from the car. They suddenly looked small and vulnerable as we turned to leave them down there. However, we knew that a crew member with responsibility for checking on them routinely during the trip was nearby. We hoped that when it became dark as the gates went up they would go to sleep, because they were exhausted from the road trip as well. We made our way up to the decks that had seating, restaurant, a small cinema, and gift shop and internet access. At this point, we lost our teenage daughter to the attractions on board, especially the internet after her endurance of hours with no stimuli on the journey so far. After having a drink and a walk around, we made our way to the reclining chairs. We had pre-booked them so that we could get some well-needed sleep during the crossing.

About three hours before we docked in Devonport we went to the restaurant for some caffeine and sustenance for the next leg of our journey. Having been too tired to notice, the crossing for our fellow passengers had been turbulent. When I went to the toilets with Jaime, there were women and children, of all ages, vomiting and looking unwell. 'Green around the gills,' as my mum used to say in her 'I told you so' tone, whenever we had over-indulged as children. As we docked in Devonport, we got our first glimpse of the state that would be our new home. True to its 'four seasons in one day' reputation it was raining: what a welcome! Fortunately, it was only a shower; by the time we disembarked, the rain stopped and the sun shone. After collecting our revived 'boys,' and enduring the hour-long queues and security checks, we were at last on the final leg of the journey

We had about a four-hour drive ahead of us, but despite some sleep on the ferry, the sleep deprivation symptoms were really kicking in. We had to make more frequent stops to keep Nigel awake and driving, until we reached our destination safely. The Tasmanian countryside is spectacular. The route from north to south takes you through picturesque towns and villages, which at the time we were unable to appreciate. Our biggest problem now was finding food, which I know sounds dramatic. However, at this stage in our Australian adventure, we were vegetarian, and for the first part of the journey I prepared snacks and meal. We now needed food urgently. After stopping at the first roadhouse, we soon realised that at the roadside Tasmania did not cater for vegetarians. Everything contained meat; even the innocent looking cheese salad roll, on closer inspection had diced bacon in the centre. As we picked the filling out of various rolls and sandwiches, we longed to find somewhere that sold at least a salad or some fruit.

Travelling across Tasmania the food situation deteriorated, and by the time we arrived at John's it was early evening and we were all hungry. He was waiting outside, in case we did not recognise the house, as it had been a couple of years since our last visit. After getting the 'boys' out and Jaime rushing indoors to charge up her mobile phone, we smiled with delight when John announced that he had dinner prepared. We ate too much, too fast and enjoyed a well-deserved glass of wine, or two, but we did not care. It was over, another interstate road trip completed, without major incident. We were home, albeit our temporary home, for the foreseeable future.

At the time of the floods, we had no idea what to expect as the process of dealing with the aftermath of the flood started to unfold. We grappled with the bureaucracy of the banks, government flood relief payments, etc. while trying to provide a stable family environment for Jaime. We should not forget that she had also lost a great deal and now had to start again in another state of Australia.

Chapter 17
The Retrieval Mission bringing 'Itchy Feet' home

Two weeks after our flood-induced relocation to Tasmania, we set out on our retrieval mission. Our treasured, 'Itchy feet,' a 1978 Toyota coaster bus, converted into a motor-home, hopefully, still sat in the woods in Millmerran, Queensland where we left it!

Itchy Feet, out home in the woods

Our project had been to 'do it up' for weekends away, but we used it as extra living space during the early stages of our preparation for our woodland retreat. Not wanting 'Itchy feet,' to be unattended in Millmerran for any longer than necessary, we made our plans to retrieve her. It would not be easy, as Nigel had driven her a mere two kilometers when we bought her. An enormous element of risk existed in attempting to move her interstate. It would be a huge challenge for the vehicle and for me, but necessary if we wanted to keep her.

To get from Hobart to Millmerran, Queensland, without a vehicle took organisation. Our trip started with domestic flights from Hobart to Sydney, followed by Sydney to Brisbane on Sunday 27th February. We booked to stay the night in a Brisbane budget hotel, to ensure catching the early morning Greyhound coach to Toowoomba. This would be followed by a second coach to Millmerran and if all went to plan, would have us in Millmerran by midday on Monday 28th February. The budget hotel turned out to be exactly that. The room did not even have a window! Cheap, but not cheerful, as soon as we entered the room, the grim darkness hit us. The room, lit by a small

Sarah Jane Butfield

circular sky light was as hot as the adjacent courtyard. Nigel at once started fiddling with the antiquated air conditioner unit and put it on full blast. As with most budget hotels, facilities were meagre, so we spent the evening flicking through a limited choice of trashy satellite television channels. With limited funds to pay for this trip, this budget hotel, despite its faults, was the only choice between having a hotel room, and sleeping at the coach station. Given that the journey ahead of us to get 'Itchy feet' home to Tasmania, would involve another road trip of over two thousand kilometres in a vehicle unable to go above 90 km/hr, we knew that we needed a good sleep.

Millmerran Woods, on the main road to Goondiwindi, is twenty-five kilometres away from the town of Millmerran. The coach driver the first, but not the last, person to offer us an act of kindness on this mission, dropped us on the outskirts of the woods instead of in the town. This left us a mere six-kilometre walk, in the midday thirty-four degree heat. We set off with our bubble-wrapped light board, undamaged despite two domestic flights and two coach trips, and our rucksacks. We had brought a change of clothes, an inverter which, for those like me who are not mechanically minded, is a gadget for converting 12 volts to 240 volts. A selection of hand tools and a bottle of water each. We were positive about our prospects for success on our mission and this kept us going.

When we arrived at the woods, it was like coming home. My two black flowerpots filled with assorted herbs still sat proudly at the entrance to the driveway. Nigel had laid a fallen tree, before we left, to deter intruders in our absence, and it looked untouched. We moved the tree and navigated our way down the driveway. It already looked overgrown in the two weeks since we had left. Memories of the trip that Jaime and I had made to see Nigel while he was retreating there after Sheila died flooded back to me. As usual, we walked along watched by the resident wildlife. I envied them, as they continued to enjoy the peace and tranquillity there.

With little water remaining and limited opportunity to find shade, as we had taken down -the structures that provided shade before we left,

134

imagine our disappointment when our beloved 'Itchy feet' refused to start. Before we left the woods for Tasmania, Nigel put the battery on trickle charge with the solar panel. However, somehow it had become dislodged and was not connected. Had those annoying cats visited again? The eye contact, with no words needed between Nigel and I said it all: 'No, this can't happen to us, not now.' We had come so far, literally, and if we could not fix it, we would have no way of getting back to Tasmania anytime soon. Despite a couple of hours of tinkering, trying to boost the battery by connecting it to another battery with dodgy wire connectors, we had to concede defeat. We had to make our first call to the Royal Automobile Club Queensland (RACQ) to arrange for a new battery to be delivered; another cost that we really did not need.

As the motor home was not covered by our membership, we had to tell a white lie and pretend that we needed it for our 4WD Nissan Pathfinder. When the mechanic arrived, we thought our plan was thwarted when he wanted to fit it for us. However, we met him at the end of the driveway and Nigel convinced him that it was not safe for his vehicle to enter. In addition, Nigel explained in detail the long arduous walk down the driveway. So much so that the RACQ call-out mechanic, who did not look like someone who enjoyed walking, happily handed over the battery for Nigel to fit. We gave him the registration details of our 4WD for his records and he left. My 'bushman' husband carried the battery down the drive effortlessly. Three hours later, with battery fitted and the engine running, we packed up and headed off on the first stage of the road trip back to Tasmania. First stop: fuel and water for the journey to Goondiwindi.

Our intention had been to get the permit to drive an unregistered vehicle on Monday afternoon, but due to the battery problem and subsequent delays, we arrived in Goondiwindi too late and had to amend our plans. The unscheduled overnight stay would enable us to be first in the queue as the Queensland Department of Transport office opened on Tuesday morning at 8.30 am. It also meant that we would need to make up the time somewhere else along the way because we already had the return ferry booked from Melbourne to Tasmania. We arrived in Goondiwindi in the evening, and parked up for the night.

The industrial area, where trucks usually parked, near to a servo (petrol station) and a McDonalds McCafe restaurant became our refuge. Our comfortable motor home bed was a welcome relief after the travels and traumas of the day. After a couple of beers for Nigel and a glass of much needed wine for me, we were quickly asleep. Tuesday morning we were up early; a hot cup of coffee from McDonald's and some food bought the previous evening from the local supermarket made us ready for the day ahead. We filled up with LPG and diesel, refilled our drinking water canisters and set off to the Department of Transport office. In preparation, we had obtained a class 22 insurance certificate, which is compulsory for the seven-day permit to be granted. Therefore, with the $182 fee, and the old registration plates removed we soon became permit holders and legally able to drive 'Itchy feet' home. The whole process efficiently completed by 9 o'clock, saw us on our way down the A39 towards Melbourne.

Our initial plan had been to drive for three days; no night driving, average speed of between 80-90 km/hr., and clocking up six to seven hours driving per day. Already behind schedule after the enforced overnight stay in Goondiwindi, on day one of the road trip we had only managed four hours driving before our plans were in question again. After a stop to use the toilet facilities in Narrabri, a small country town in New South Wales, we pulled out into a busy junction of the A39 where 'Itchy feet' decided to stop. With only a clicking noise, when attempting a restart, a degree of panic ensued. With huge road-trains coming in both directions and busy lunchtime traffic, we needed a miracle. Road-trains, used for freight transportation, consist of a truck with two or three trailers attached.

Our second act of kindness came from a workman who, seeing our plight, pulled his 4WD vehicle up behind 'Itchy feet' and set his hazard lights flashing. He helped me to push 'Itchy feet,' backwards from the front, so that Nigel could steer her towards the kerb out of danger. Pushing a mere 2.5 tonnes of converted bus, yes, I should have sat in the driver's seat and done the steering, but my nerves were shot. I just could not do it. As luck would have it, an undulation in the road, helped 'Itchy feet' roll the last few feet into position, and the traffic flow resumed around us on the A39.

The temperature outside, thirty-six degrees, but in the motor-home, making telephone calls with the windows closed due to heavy traffic noise, it must have been nearer to forty degrees. The sweat ran down our faces, arms and backs. Frustration and anxiety flowed through me. Why wouldn't just one thing go to plan, just one thing be easy, just for once. My positivity had deserted me momentarily as I stood on the kerb, and Nigel gave our details over the telephone. I did not want to go any further, but I did not want to be here either. My PTSD was kicking in; I had to try to get it back under control. Nigel had enough to worry about without me freaking out on him.

Our call was now diverted to the National Roads & Motorists association (NRMA) roadside assist, as we were in NSW. (RACQ equivalent) This resulted in a very prompt response unit arriving just thirty minutes later. The technician examined our motor home. Some chin rubbing, head scratching, and battery testing followed, before the conclusion was made that with the battery new yesterday, the problem should be the starter motor. The mechanic called for backup from another NRMA mechanic, due to the size of our vehicle. When a second driver arrived, the plan to try to tow start 'Itchy feet' into the busy A39 traffic went into action.

The noise and vibration from the passing traffic filled me with fear. We were sitting ducks, waiting to be hit by a passing car, or worse, a road-train. However, we could do nothing about it. Nigel, amazingly calm as always, took control and reassured me constantly. Being towed into the traffic, I wanted to close my eyes: I really did not want to look. Imagine our relief when the engine started, and the roar of the accelerator rang through our ears. We smiled at each other as the engine stayed running, as we pulled over to let the tow ropes release. We were given strict instructions 'not to turn the engine off' until we reached the auto electricians workshop which was located a couple of kilometres away. All of our hopes now lay with this auto electrician, and that he may be able to help us. We were on our way, albeit somewhat gingerly for fear of stopping or stalling the engine.

The auto electrician workshop, a small family-based business, operated from a large shed in his garden. We looked at each other and knew that we were both thinking, 'what the hell is this?' This is not a garage that can fix a bus. Contrary to our first impressions, it had an organised workshop, and they offered an extremely helpful and efficient service. As instructed, Nigel manoeuvred 'Itchy feet' into their garden, and drove it to the rear of the workshop. This must have looked very strange, a bus converted to a motor home being driven around the garden near to their washing line as it spun in the breeze. Nigel parked 'Itchy feet,' and as instructed did not turn off the engine. As we walked away from her, we now hoped she would not overheat sitting there. If the engine stalled there was no room to tow start it as before. The auto electrician, estimating that it would take at least a couple of hours to repair, as they had to wait for the engine to cool down, suggested we go and wait somewhere cooler and have some lunch. We accepted his advice, as the intense heat and stress began taking its toll on us now. He drove us to a local pub with air conditioning to wait while they worked on 'Itchy feet.'

This was a surreal experience for us. Having only been in Australia for three years, Nigel and I still sounded very English. Therefore, walking into a country pub and requesting two diet cokes with ice, caused a few raised eyebrows. The local old guys at the bar were sipping ice-cold beer and betting on Keno and the Grafton races via satellite, as the women were taking turns to reserve the pokies, (slot machines) while they waited for more change from the bar. We looked and felt out of place, but we took our seats and pretended to make polite chit chat, people-watching those around us. Two hours passed; we took a walk from the pub to the nearby shop and bought some salad rolls, and then returned to the air-conditioned pub for more diet cokes and respite from the heat. A storm brewed up outside, making the palm trees creak and bend as the wind swirled and shook the long branches. Then, one of the auto electricians called to say he would collect us: at last some news. Pleased and grateful we found 'Itchy feet' fixed and her engine running, and at reasonable rates considering the amount of time and the parts required. Now we would try again to go home.

Back on the road again, but having lost about four hours travelling time, we pondered our travel plans once more. As darkness descended, it was unsafe to continue. Although we did so for a while, because Nigel, 'being Nigel' or 'just being a man', always wanted to push it a little bit further. The events of the day, which had been stressful and exhausting, caught up with us and tiredness consumed our minds and bodies. We decided to find a place to camp for the night, and a lay-by at the side of the A39 served this purpose. One of the good things about Australian highways is that there are plenty of lay-bys and they cater well for travellers. After some much-needed food, sleep beckoned.

At 4.30 am, a jolting sensation and loud engine noise woke me. Nigel had decided to try to catch up on our schedule by setting off during the night, as I slept. I do not know how far he had driven, but I was soon sitting in the passenger seat, rubbing the sleep from my eyes, still in my pyjamas checking my map book. The new plan was to make up time by making shorter stops and therefore covering more kilometres throughout the day. Nigel performed like a robot; I kept him fed, watered and talked 'crap' to keep him awake, to enable us to keep going. He just kept driving, not wanting to stop or look at anything. We were on a mission; then suddenly we saw the signs for Melbourne. Now we had ended up on the outskirts of Melbourne a day ahead of schedule. How did that happen?

Not wanting to be hanging around in the Melbourne CBD, we telephoned the 'Spirit of Tasmania' ferry office to see if we could move our ferry booking forward. Fortunately, we were able to move to the morning ferry, meaning we would arrive in Tasmania on Thursday evening instead of Friday. After a short toilet break, we did our routine check of the light board and discovered we now had no brake lights!

"I wonder how far we have travelled like that." Nigel said,

exasperated that something else had now gone wrong.

We tentatively started making our way into Melbourne with no brake lights. With a detour in place, and the evening rush hour traffic to contend with there was no option except to keep going. Utilising Nigel's ingenious plan of flicking the lights on and off when braking, to imitate brake lights, we eventually made it to the port. We must have flashed so many drivers, because of the front lights coming on and off as well, during this technique to achieve brake lights.

There are limited free parking spaces at Melbourne ferry port, but we managed to grab a good spot, ready for the morning ferry queue. Other camper-vans parked up around us, together with the odd car with its driver looking uncomfortable, trying to sleep. We knew that feeling well, from our recent road trip. As we sat with our cold beer and wine, we pondered what sort of journey the people around us had experienced to get there, betting it was nothing like ours! We were nearly home.

The early morning ferry boarded with efficiency, just as it had done when we had travelled with the 4WD and trailer. 'Itchy feet' behaved and even made short work of the steep ramps onto the loading deck. Some young backpackers shouted over to say how awesome our vehicle was. This brought a smile to our faces; she had character and we loved her. We felt a bit more at ease now that we were on the homeward stretch. Once we were on Tasmanian soil, if anything else happened it would be easier to get her towed home. The remainder of the journey was uneventful, apart from the fact that we still had no brake lights. That aside 'Itchy feet' had taken us home; in return, we would restore her into a fully functioning motor home. 'Itchy feet' looked in a sorry state right now, covered in flies of all descriptions, a true array of multi-state bugs. As for us, we were looking a bit sorry for ourselves too, minus the flies, but with lots more grey hairs!

Chapter 18
Restarting our Australian Adventure

So here we were in Tasmania, the southernmost state of Australia. With a climate that is, changeable, often described as four seasons in one day. The weather more similar to that in the UK than anywhere else we had lived in Australia, at least a degree of familiarity existed. Tasmania is a picturesque state with tourism as its main industry. Our first priority was to find work. Without anywhere permanent to live, we had no scope to build a business and re-establish ourselves. Therefore, the vicious circle of finding a job to be able to rent a house commenced.

However close your relationship is with your family, moving them in with your parents, in your forties, is not always easy. When the realisation that it is not a holiday is acknowledged, added to the psychological and emotional stress that put you there, the result is a roller-coaster ride of emotions and tension. Most of us expect that when we fly the nest, as young adults in our late teens or early twenties, to live and become independent, that the visits to our parents in the future would be for holidays and special occasions. Or, in later life to assist them as they deal with the onset of old age. Therefore, you can imagine that to have to return to live, and be dependent on, your father was one of the very hardest times for Nigel to endure. However, until we found new employment and somewhere to rent, John's support was vital. We remain enormously grateful for the generosity and willingness that John showed us as he opened his house to three extra people and two dogs. However, living in someone else's house is hard. While they go out to work, you struggle to get a job interview, despite numerous qualifications and experience. The experience was depressing and intolerable at times. What we needed was a new focus, but with the financial reality of the flood facing us every day, we could only focus on short-term goals. As clichéd as it may sound now, my new focus became my writing. I had started two diploma writing courses, via distance learning, when we were in Queensland; therefore, I used this additional enforced free time to study hard on my assignments. In part, this was to distract me from the harsh reality of our circumstances. In addition, it would give me something, in the future, to aim for. I now know that the writing of my journals during that time helped me to steer my writing career in a more positive direction. I became able to write from my heart, with confidence.

With true grit and determination to restart our life, we both started looking for work, enduring many knock-backs and disappointments along the way. Nigel had started job-hunting online in the woods before we left Queensland. He applied to the Tasmanian Police, which were recruiting at that time. He completed various stages of the application process including forms, references, medical questionnaire, and after we arrived an assessment day, etc. before being disappointed when government funding was withdrawn. They put a stop to the recruitment of all new officers for that financial year. However, Nigel's biggest disappointment came in the form of receiving this news just after being informed that he had passed the assessment day screening tests so he would have been a police recruit.

When one door closed, he looked for another, and turned his attention to what he knew best, security. He completed the process of transferring his security licence from the Northern Territory to Tasmania after completing a couple of updates. Finally, securing a job with a local security company doing night patrols, we had the first piece of the new puzzle, and our new journey would start making some progress.

In the meantime, I struggled with job-hunting. With transport for shift work a problem as John lived a good forty-minute drive from the nearest general hospital, I decided to look for any job. I applied for shop work, admin, farm work, etc. However, I soon found out that in order to get a foot in the door, I had to take all my experience off my résumé. It became obvious to me, after receiving rejection feedback, that I was too experienced in nursing and management for these jobs. Feeling dejected, that my years of hard work, skills and learning meant nothing, when all I wanted was to help get us re-established I took on board what they said. I looked at my experience and skills and decided to broaden the job search. Maybe I should go back into nurse agency work, who knows, but I would find something. I saw a position advertised with a global insurance company for an injury management coordinator, (IMC,) and not really knowing what this meant or entailed, I set about researching it. The application process was arduous and took several months, but by May, I was employed and it was a relief. Working full-time, Monday to Friday office hours as an IMC, was the perfect combination for all of us. I had evenings free to be with Jaime to help her settle into another new school, with new friends, etc., and time with Nigel when he had an evening off.

The IMC role was amazing; it pushed my knowledge and expertise to the limits, but that was the appeal. With every case being different, and the result being to try to coordinate the efficient provision of medical resources to get injured workers returned to work, in some form, after an accident or work related illness, as quickly as possible. Workers got the best care: fast consultations with specialists and excellent allied healthcare support. The small team of people who I worked with in the Hobart office were long-standing employees, the sign of a good employer. We also worked closely with the team in Launceston, the Tasmanian head office. Some of the staff had been there over twenty years, and the state manager had been there forty years! Perfect, now we were in a position to rent a house and become a 'normal' family again.

We initially rented a small house not far from John's in a place called Boomer Bay. It had picturesque estuary views from its double aspect windows. On a corner plot, there was plenty of room for 'our boys.' However, the neighbours had teenaged sons that enjoyed 'hooning,' which is racing cars up and down the lanes. This did not bode well for Nigel, sleeping during the day after a twelve-hour night shift. In addition, as it was winter, the remoteness and the poor travelling conditions made us realise that, with both of us working full-time in Hobart, we needed to move to the suburbs. Moving closer to our work would also solve the issues of transport to and from work, with our beloved 4WD about to be claimed as an asset in the bankruptcy proceedings. It would also help my PTSD, because to avoid driving in the city I used to drive to the nearby town of Sorrel and catch a bus to work. This added three hours of commuting to my working day and the anxiety experienced every day, getting to and from the bus stop, was extreme.

One morning, it was very icy: I was driving cautiously in the dark along Arthur Highway, which is renowned for accidents during bad weather. A car pulled out of the Primrose Sands junction ahead of me, and as I turned the next corner that car was on its roof. I stopped the car and jumped out: luckily, my adrenaline and nursing skills kicked in and my concern was for the driver, who was able to scramble out, and not for myself. His dad had been following and pulled up behind me and soon took over the situation, thanking me for my assistance. I returned to my car, but did not want to get in. I was on my way to work, I knew I had to go but I just froze. After finding the courage to get in the car, I sat for a while. Unable to, and with no desire to, start the engine, I shivered in the cold morning air with no heater for warmth. Then, hearing and realising emergency vehicles were approaching, and would need to pull in, I started the car and drove. I must have been in autopilot, because in all honesty I do not remember the remainder of the journey to the bus stop. I could not do this anymore.

In September, we rented a lovely split-level house in the suburb of Howrah, twenty minutes to the beach and only a fifteen-minute bus ride to the CBD where I worked. It was an open plan, four-bedroom house that had a good garden space for our boys and plenty of room for Nigel to make a gym and for me to have a writing room. No more driving for me, and it was wonderful, like a huge weight had been lifted from me. Jaime could walk to school and she had access to a social life, making good friends and joining the local church youth group.

To achieve something positive from our Tasmanian experience we decided that we would each take up a hobby; something we had always wanted to do, but had never made the time to pursue. Nigel focused on his photography and his running. Tasmania is a very picturesque and environmentally diverse state. It has a variety of beaches, mountains and forests. The beaches, especially those in secluded areas with limited access, lend themselves to amazing photographs of wind-blown sand dunes, and a variety of seashells. Inland, the array of plant life and trees, scattered with old sheep sheds and rusty fencing, gave him amazing photographic opportunities. However, his night-time city traffic shots and beautifully lit old government buildings photographed were spectacular too.

He re-started his running by competing in ten-kilometre fun runs. Firstly competing in the Burnie 10, and Devonport 10, races before moving up to the Cadbury's half-marathon. From then on, he went into endurance racing, with the prestigious, 'Point to Pinnacle' race up Mount Wellington as his first experience. This is no mean feat: running twenty two kilometres up a mountain starting in the sunshine then running through rain, sleet and ending in snow at the peak. I am always so proud, supporting him at the start and finish lines. The running gave him a buzz, he is good at it, and it inspired Jaime to start competing as well, at the ten-kilometre fun run level.

Mount Wellington towers above Hobart, like a mother watching over her children. It can be seen from the suburbs and from the office blocks in the city. The changing colours during the day, and throughout the seasons, are always a talking point. The peak is often sprinkled in snow, even in the summertime. Nearer the base, the slopes are wooded, and a maze of walking tracks and fire trails lend themselves to ramblers, runners and cyclists. From the city, a narrow road of about twenty-one kilometres takes you to the summit. The peak sits approximately four thousand feet above the harbour. Mount Wellington offers a mountain experience just minutes' drive of the CBD and a favourite with locals and tourists.

I was diagnosed with early degenerative bone disease in my knees shortly after arriving in Tasmania, but thought it was just the colder climate compared to Alice Springs and Queensland. I became determined that I would do something to halt this, as I still have too much to do in my life to be limited by my mobility. Therefore, after taking professional advice from my doctor, physiotherapist and a personal trainer I decided that my new positive mission would be to get fit and slow down the disease process. For the first time in my life, I joined a gym, which resulted in an eight kilograms weight loss. I concentrated on strengthening my muscles to support my weakened joints. I also started to 'blog' about my experiences in order to help and motivate others in my predicament. Working in the CBD meant I could go to the gym before work and at lunchtime without encroaching on our family life. The physical and psychological impact was amazing. I regained my self-confidence, I became strong physically and mentally, and it felt good. My highlight was becoming strong enough to complete the 'City to Casino,' eleven-kilometre fun run with my family.

Tasmania is a tourist hot spot for many very good reasons. It has unspoilt coastlines, mountain ranges, a variety of woodlands and forests and offers an array of caravan and camping locations for travellers of all ages. The coastline near to John's house consists of Marion Bay, a haven for wild birds and pelicans that congregate on the coastal spit and are unperturbed by careful visitors.

Marion bay, Tasmania

Marion Bay is a special place in our hearts as we visited there for the first time with Sheila on our first visit to Australia. It's a place we have been back to many times, especially during the period when we were living with John, as it is only minutes away from his house.

Sheila loved walking the beach and collecting shells, and every time we go there we feel close to her. Despite the changeable weather patterns, Tasmania offers all year round tourist locations, from skiing in the mountains, wild camping along the coast as well as a variety of fishing opportunities for boat, beach and river anglers.

We took advantage of some of the many free sightseeing attractions such as Snug Falls – where Nigel took some amazing waterfall photographs. Mayfield Conservation Reserve, which offers a free campsite located beside the beach. From here, you can see seals and dolphins, when in season, from your tent or caravan door. Our boys, Dave and Buster, loved camping there, it is dog friendly and the beach lends itself as a great area for dog exercising, in specified areas to protect the wildlife. Therefore, with life resembling some form of normality, to the outside world we were coping well with our circumstances. Inside though, we were both struggling, but we are not quitters and we would not concede, so we battled on to build a new life.

As time passed for us after the flood, life had not been straightforward for one of our children in the UK. Samantha, who we had last seen at her wedding in the January 2011, had unfortunately had to deal with the fact that her new marriage was a sham. After becoming separated within a couple of months of getting married, and with us unable to visit her because of the bankruptcy restrictions, she decided to come to Tasmania. She applied for a one-year working holiday visa, so she could take some time out to decide how to move on with her life. In November, Samantha arrived to live with us. After the breakdown of her marriage, she needed the warmth and comfort of her family, and that is exactly what we gave her. She needed to laugh, to cry, and do new things and she needed her family. She found work as a waitress and came alive again; ready to start a new chapter in her life and put her heartache and disappointment behind her.

Samantha arrives in Hobart:
Sarah Jane with Samantha and Jaime on Howrah beach

Nigel worked on his career, and despite working full-time as a security guard, he retrained as a private investigator. He loved this work, especially as he is a bit nosey! For a better work-life balance, and to get more time to work freelance as a P.I., he found a position as a member of the security team at the Wrest Point Hotel Casino on the waterfront.

The Wrest Point Hotel opened in December 1939. Enjoying its heyday during the war, it was later sold to the Federal Hotel Group, Australia's oldest hotel chain, in 1956. In an attempt to secure Australia's first casino licence the group claimed that a casino would help develop Tasmania as a tourist attraction. In addition, as Tasmania's scenery and natural beauty were not widely accessible or known about the idea struck a chord. A state referendum had to be held, due to the controversy over the issue of the first casino licence; however it was granted. The casino complex was developed with a seventeen-storey hotel tower, which contains a revolving restaurant. This now iconic tower is often representative of Hobart, and it remains the tallest building in Hobart at sixty-four metres in height. The casino launch, and its on-going presence, continues to boost and support Tasmanian tourism.

Nigel was very good, and proficient, at both jobs and was soon offered a promotion to supervisor at the casino. He turned it down at first, as he preferred to be one of the lads. He liked the 'hands on' work, walking the casino floors, removing patrons who were inappropriate in their behaviour and those who were banned or underage. He made some good, life-long friends at the casino. This combination of jobs made him happy, because he had the time to take his interest in photography more seriously. Even when he was on a P.I assignment, he would take any opportunity, in the many wonderful locations around Tasmania, to get that elusive perfect photograph.

My working life fitted in really well with home life. I would go to work, go the gym after work and be home for family dinner when Jaime got in from school. In the school holidays, Jaime and or Samantha would meet me for lunch and we would walk to the harbour and eat, overlooking the fishing boats and expensive yachts manoeuvring in and out of the marina. My friends from work gave a new support to me as an individual. At work, I was respected for my knowledge and skills, but I was valued as a friend. We would often lunch or drink coffee in the array of bars, coffee houses and restaurants within walking distance of the office, putting the world to rights. We laughed a lot, supported each other when one or other of our children were in hospital or having teenage troubles and we made a good team at work.

Nigel and I accepted not being able to buy another house. Not having credit cards or owning anything over five thousand dollars in value did not concern us either. What really pulled at our heart-strings, and which stopped this from being the perfect life, which it now should have been, were the restriction of the bankruptcy. This stopped us from travelling freely. Moreover, when some of your children live on the other side of the world, you like to think that if the time came and they needed you, then you would get a flight and go. This is not the case although you can apply for permission to travel for emergencies, it is not the same as having the ability to do it without questions being asked. In addition, we could not holiday to the UK, and ok we could not afford it, but it was the principal that we just could not do it if we wanted to.

With the bankruptcy finalised and the worry of that process behind us, well apart from the restrictions, we were free to start to enjoy Australia again and we tried to accept the restrictions and continue to live the Australian dream.

Chapter 19
It's Christmas! Tasmanian style

What can I say? Christmas over the four years since we left the UK had taken us through a disorderly range of emotions and misgivings. Twice, we had spent Christmas lonely in Alice Springs. We had spent one wonderful Christmas in the UK visiting all of our children, only to come back to find our house had been flooded. This year, Christmas 2011, was our first in Tasmania as bankrupts, which although it does not affect Christmas, hangs over you like a dark cloud. There had to be some 'positive spin' that we could apply to this, surely.

My positive spin was that this, the first Christmas since the flood, was also our first Christmas spent in Australia with two of our children present – Samantha and Jaime. With the ghosts of Christmas past haunting us, we decided to break with tradition and go camping by the sea for the Christmas weekend. With John in his camper van and me, Nigel, Jaime and Samantha in three tents, our accommodation was sorted. The 'boys,' of course, would have the luxury of the backseat of Samantha's car because they needed a bit of comfort!

Our plan was to head off on Christmas Eve, after work, and camp at the free camp site at Mayfield Reserve, on the East Coast of Tasmania, a two-hour drive from Hobart. We had been there a few times before and we loved it. At Mayfield, you can camp with dogs, free of charge, and it is not formalised with allocated pitches. It welcomes campers of all types, from tents to caravans, backpackers to converted buses and motor homes. We saw some wonderful motor homes there, and it inspired us to save some money to work on restoring our precious 'Itchy feet.' We saw groups of fishermen with their 'tinnies'. This slang term has many connotations, but in this context, it is Australian slang for small metal boats, which can be launched from the beach. They connect on the tow bar of your vehicle, so they are quick and ready for action. Fishermen and their families meet up at Mayfield Conservation Reserve for a weekend of fishing, BBQ's and alcohol-induced hilarity, as is the Australian tradition. Reunions of families and friends are often found taking over a big corner of the site.

The only facilities at Mayfield are two dunnies, where you have to be vigilant for spiders, especially huntsman and red backs, under the seat or inside the toilet roll at any time of year. Whatever the occasion, the sense of community at Mayfield is extended to all. Everyone acknowledges one another with a courteous 'G'day' or 'How ya going?' Some, noticing the pomme accent, will enquire with 'Where ya from?' When you say the UK they reply with, 'Oh you're from London', because isn't that where everyone in the UK comes from! A keen nation of dog lovers they often ask what breed of dog you have, etc., but not in a nosey way. It is in a like-minded, friendly and welcoming way. We liked this and we really started to believe that we could be 'at home' in Tasmania.

Tasmania has so much to offer families and individuals who enjoy the outdoors, as we do. The variety of coastal locations around the island is spectacular and easily accessible. There is an array of isolated spots, where you can sit and watch seals, dolphins and other wildlife, depending on the season. It has some of the best fishing locations in the world and a vast array of photography opportunities. For example, Wine Glass Bay, another iconic Tasmanian location, and one place that we visited. It takes your breath away, literally, with the walk to the ridge, the spectacular view and its natural beauty. With so many plus points to our new homeland, it was hard to find any negatives.

We met up with John in Hobart and set off as planned in convoy, one camper and two cars. With walkie-talkies and CB radio contact between our vehicles, because of too much chatter the batteries were worn out after only half-an-hour's driving! The weather, being summertime was glorious and we were excited to experience our first beach Christmas. Although, we were not together as a family, somehow this felt right, for once. I suppose we have always liked to do things a bit differently; we are spontaneous and sometimes, in other people's eyes, irresponsible. However, as a beach Christmas in the UK is never a real option, unless you want to dress up in coats and blankets in the wind, rain or snow, we decided we had to experience it, even if only once; a bucket list item I think.

Here on the East Coast of Tasmania, in the early evening we had temperatures of twenty-five degrees, with a lovely sea breeze as evening approached in an orange glow ahead of us on the horizon. The problem with glorious conditions is that many others had the same idea, and when we arrived at Mayfield Reserve we found it packed to the rafters: no room at the inn on Christmas Eve, a bit like the nativity, but without the pregnant woman!

Our convoy reconvened in a lay-by to discuss our options. Some may consider it somewhat irresponsible that we had not considered this scenario, and had not researched any other sites that would allow dogs. We decided that John, Samantha and Jaime would stay at the lay-by while Nigel and I would drive on to Swansea, the next biggest seaside town on the East coast, to check out the campsites there. The first one we came to, which had three spaces available, did not allow dogs on the site, which was not helpful. The next site was full until New Year. We sat in the car debating our next move; with evening fast approaching. We still had to set up camp when we found somewhere. With multiple vehicles and dogs, this is not an ideal scenario. We could either drive further risking the same responses or go back. Time ticked on and conscious that wherever we chose to go we needed to get there soon, the pressure mounted.

We drove back to where we left the others, to discuss our options. Now Nigel's slightly devious side reared its head: being Christmas Eve he thought that the probability of the park wardens, that patrol the 'day-camping only' sites, being at work was remote. Therefore, we decided to take a chance and go to Spikey Beach, just a couple of kilometres away from Mayfield Reserve.

We loved this area of coastline. However, the issue is you are not supposed to camp there. When we arrived, the light was fading and one car sat parked with no occupants. It looked like it belonged to a couple of young lads, judging by the McDonald's empty packets and Red Bull cans scattered inside. Perhaps they were having an evening of fishing off from the beach. We decided we would wait until they left, which would probably be soon if they were law-abiding young

153

lads, unlike us.

We would then set up our tents behind John's camper van, so that they were not visible from the road. We had cooking facilities in the camper, so we had no need to light fires, therefore we posed no fire risk to the wildlife and habitat around us. According to plan, the young lads left before darkness descended, and we erected our tents, and settled down to watch the last of the sunset over a few cold beers and some Chardonnay for the girls. Christmas Eve looking out to sea was idyllic, peaceful and it felt amazing.

Christmas Eve illegally camping at a secret beach location

Christmas morning and Nigel was first up, as always, and he went off for a walk to the beach leaving us all sleeping in our tents. As I started to stir, I could hear Nigel talking to Jaime. He had spotted a pod of dolphins just off the shore and had come back for his camera: what a treat, 'Merry Christmas' from a pod of dolphins playing just metres from the shore.

Nigel took some amazing photographs, and later Samantha and John were annoyed that they had missed the dolphins. We walked on the beach to find a spot to put up a pagoda for some shade under which we would have our Christmas feast.

Christmas Day – tents safely hidden.

We marked out a space in the sand to dig a fire pit for our Christmas Day, BBQ lunch. We had bought an array of seafood, for the vegetarians, and meat for John, Samantha and Jaime, plus salad and bubbly to toast our first Christmas in Tasmania. As we climbed the bank back to the campervan to get the provisions, guess who was walking towards us? Yes, you guessed it, the park wardens, at midday on Christmas Day! Who would have thought that councils would pay treble time for them to patrol the day-camping spaces, but they did.

They greeted us with, "G'Day, Happy Christmas."

"How ya going? Merry Christmas", Nigel said in his pomme, Australian accent.

I suppose the tents and camping gear had been a giveaway that we were illegally camping there. Anyway, Nigel explained our plight about expecting to camp at Mayfield and that no other sites were accepting dogs nearby.

"Well, as its Christmas and you've probably already had a drink to celebrate," wink, wink, "it would be wrong of us to move you on. So how about you take down the tents and put them up again later. We don't want to encourage others to join you".

After Nigel promised that we would head off the next day, they let

155

us off without a fine, 'as its Christmas,' for which we were very grateful. We took down the tents and then returned to the beach for our Christmas lunch. Later that day, just before dusk, we set up our make shift camp site again for another perfect night's camping. It was so special being there together as a family; we wanted to enjoy our whole Christmas Day, but we would leave as promised in the morning. Our Christmas lunch was a family-cooked affair, with everyone taking a turn at cooking prawn skewers, fish, steaks etc. A lot of laughter and hilarity prevailed, especially as the bubbly flowed and John fell off his camping chair, luckily into the soft sand around us.

During the day, we fished from the rocks with Jaime catching the first fish, but with Nigel catching the biggest fish of the day, of course. As we were still quite short of money after the flood-induced relocation, funds were short, so the Christmas present plan was that everyone would pick a name from the hat and would buy for that person only, thus ensuring everyone received a gift. A twenty-dollar limit was set to avoid overzealous shoppers, namely Samantha and John, from getting carried away. It was lovely to see how creative it made us all: for example, Nigel received a photo frame made from a silver cake plate Samantha had bought from Vinnie's, a charity shop, like the Salvation Army. She had glued photographs of 'our boys' to it and decorated it in seashells from Marion Bay. This meant more than any expensive shop-bought gift. Jaime received a small wooden box decorated with her name in glitter, just the right size to hold cotton wool pads for makeup removal, and some toiletries to assist in that process. Nigel had made John a clock with an old LP record as the clock face, something he still treasures, and it hangs with pride in his dining room. It is a talking point for people who visit him, as he recounts the story of our Tasmanian Christmas camping trip.

So finally, we had achieved an Australian Christmas, without loneliness. We had laughed, enjoyed good unpretentious food and wine, and Nigel and I still managed to speak to all of our children, except Molly. It was quite strange to be standing on the beach in the afternoon heat saying, "Happy Christmas", on a mobile phone to our children twelve thousand miles away. We talked out about their

Christmas Day so far and gifts etc., and let them know that we were
thinking of them and missed them so much.

As planned, at first light Boxing Day morning, we packed up and
drove down the road to Mayfield Reserve to see if it had thinned out
over the Christmas Day. It was still full and very crowded, so we
parked for a few hours in the day-parking there, to enjoy the beach and
to exercise the boys before returning home. Regardless of the logistical
hiccups Christmas had been more than just 'OK' this year, it had been
fun, and we made memories that will be reminisced about for many
years to come. Then again, is it a proper Christmas without the snow,
cold temperatures, Father Christmas suits and drinking mulled wine
around the fire? Or seeing a robin, doing what robins do in your
garden over winter. Is this what we were really missing at Christmas in
Australia, tradition?

So did we dare contemplate where we would be for Christmas
2012? No. The furthest we were able to look forward this Christmas
was into 2012.

We had moved into a new house in September 2011. Samantha had
arrived in November and was living with us. Her new partner Cam
would be joining her, from the UK, in January 2012 to travel around
Australia with her. Cam was an old friend, with whom she had
rekindled a relationship in the months after she separated from her
husband, before coming out to Australia. We were living in Tasmania,
trying to rebuild our lives after the flood. We were doing it. It was
slow, and hard, but we knew that we could and would do it.

Our positivity motivated us to believe in ourselves, and the fact that
we would get our lives back on track, so that we could start dreaming
again. What was our new dream going to be? I had a little dream of
saving up and visiting Sydney for New Year 2012 to see the fireworks
over the Sydney Opera House. Longer term, I wanted to save up to
visit Italy after the bankruptcy conditions ended in September 2015.
Nigel's dream was to renovate 'Itchy feet,' so that we could travel
around Australia when we took holidays from work. We needed to

continue our Australian dream and experience the culture and diversity of this amazing country.

So is this it, is Tasmania our home for the future? Can we put down our 'roots' here? Do we even have 'roots?' Nigel's parents were in the Army. He was born in Hong Kong, before they moved to Northern Ireland and Germany, twice, for tours of duty. Moving has never bothered or fazed him, in fact he enjoys it! 'Wherever I lay my hat, that's my home', is his saying. For me, well I think I must come from gypsy stock, because although I can't say I enjoy the moving, I do fall in love easily with new places, and sometimes I take my 'carpe diem'(seize the day) far too literally. However, I must be getting old because I feel the need to put down some roots, but I do not know if this is the right place. Are there too many missing pieces or people?

Can we, should we, will we?

The answer is …………………………………….. In Chapter 20

Chapter 20
Homesick – it's decision time

Reality strikes

Sadly, the final part of the floods impact arrived when we had to declare ourselves voluntarily bankrupt. After months of letters, emails, telephone calls, appointments with debt counsellors, etc. the harsh reality dawned. We had a house, now worth less than the mortgage on it: unable to raise the money to repair the flood damage, or at least stabilise the property, and with no flood insurance, we had few options remaining. Despite us now working full-time, the debt that had accrued since the flood was now insurmountable. The time had come to draw a line under our Australian property dream.

The trustees would take the flood-ravaged house, as it stood, in Ipswich. Our twenty acres of woodland in Millmerran, and our beloved 4WD Nissan pathfinder, which had taken us on many adventures, but more damaging was that our dignity and self-respect were in tatters. It imposes restrictions and implications on your life, in a very public and obvious way. You find yourself having to declare it on the most random occasions. For us, with the majority of our children overseas, the restrictions on travel became the hardest consequence to come to terms with. However much I tried, my positive spin was in short supply to aid our current situation. We were fortunate, we were alive and well, but life is only worth living when your basic needs are met. Being able to go to our children when they need us is a basic need, and not a luxury.

As well as the bankruptcy proceedings being finalised at this time, coincidentally the personal injury claim proceedings from the road rage incident in April 2010 were also approaching a court hearing. It was all too much; I didn't care anymore. I would not travel to Queensland alone, to sit like a criminal in court opposite the man who had, in many ways, ruined my life. Overly dramatic, possibly, but my loss of confidence, and my loss of independence from not driving, all meant a great deal to me and no amount of compensation would change that. When I informed the legal team of my decision not to go ahead, they urged me to reconsider. With a 'no win, no fee' arrangement they get nothing if I get nothing. Therefore, they hastily set up a mediation conference call, to see if an out of court settlement could be reached, as it was over two years since the accident.

On the day of the conference call, I took the day off work. This would be traumatic, and even if I didn't have to see anyone, it would upset me just talking about it. The call as expected was an agonising experience: listening to his legal representative belittling my symptoms, trying to blame my issues on the flood, instead of the accident. They disputed the medical evidence, from not only the psychological assessment, but also the medical reports in relation to the whiplash injury, etc. I wanted it to end. Throughout the call, whenever they went off to confer and make up figures to offer, etc., I had to sit on the telephone listening to dreadful music, which circled on a loop as they took so long. When the final offer came, my legal team advised that if I changed my mind and went to court they said, 'we could achieve at least four to six times this amount.' Not interested in the money, I would have accepted the very first offer of the day, if it had just been me talking. I just wanted to finish it. Anyway, the relief of hanging up from that call was immense. Shaking, and physically sick, as my body acknowledged the relief that washed over me during those first few minutes. Crying, but not through sadness; exhausted, but not through exercise, I sat rooted to the chair. Eager to tell Nigel, I sat and waited for him to come home.

It would be over three months before the final statement arrived, after they worked out the costs to be deducted for assessments, travel etc., and their fees, of course. The result being that three months later the statement said that I would receive forty thousand dollars in approximately three months' time. I informed the bankruptcy trustee, who confirmed that the compensation, not classed as an asset that would be taken, was protected, together with anything that I bought with it. What would we do with it?

The implications of the voluntary bankruptcy over the next three years would control our visits to the UK to see our children. We would have to ask for permission to see our own children, justifying the reason, a most abnormal, unnatural sensation. In my twenty-five years of being a parent, I had never felt like this. I didn't feel like a proper mum anymore. When your children need you, you go - that is all there is to it. We realised then that our Australian adventure had run its course.

As we tried to come to terms with the bankruptcy restrictions, we were homesick for the first time; it hit us both in a very grand style. We tried to reassure ourselves that the children would visit us and that in an emergency the trustees would grant us permission to go to them. The reality was that we did not want someone else to be in control of that aspect of our life. We were homesick, not for the UK, but for the children. We wanted - we needed - to have access and closeness to our family, our children and their lives.

At this point in time, what are we trying to achieve by staying in Australia? Are we trying to prove a point that our initial decision to emigrate remained justified, that we had made the right decision then? To us, none of that mattered now. We had emigrated; we had achieved and experienced wonderful things during our four and half years in Australia, and we had experienced good and challenging times. Despite this we stood firm as a family unit; still together, still wanting more adventures, more challenges, but now we were suffocating in circumstance. Trapped and unable to be free spirits, with our trademark unpredictability gone. Our life had been tamed, restricted, and we were not the same people anymore.

We have always enjoyed travel whether it is for pleasure, for work or education. With this in mind, we initially tried to set ourselves a three-year plan for when the travel restrictions would be lifted. We started by organising a mini break of four days to Hervey Bay in Queensland for February, arriving on Valentine's Day.

Hervey Bay, Queensland

It was somewhere we had always wanted to go when we lived in Queensland and so now we had some money, we decided a romantic trip away was just what the doctor ordered. The amazingly spectacular scenery with clear blue skies, miles of sandy beaches, and an array of restaurants and coffee shops was more than enough to meet anyone's tastes. In addition to all of this, we had an apartment overlooking the sea with a Jacuzzi on the balcony. Paradise at last: Australia had something to offer us after all. We were free to travel throughout Australia unrestricted, so was this the answer? After a wonderful four days, we returned to Tasmania, invigorated and eager to move on to find new adventures to have, and to enjoy life.

Aim for 2014 became the goal. We made a dream board to hang in the kitchen with places we wanted to visit in Italy; places we wanted to go with the children, and as couple. Nothing was out of bounds, we could dream big. In reality, though 2014, to us, was a lifetime away. I know that as you get older time is supposed to appear to go faster, and trust me as I write this today I sense the time passing very quickly. However, with such long-term restrictions ahead of us, each day was a month, each month a year and 2014 an unachievable goal.

My positivity waned again, until one night over dinner. We were discussing visiting Italy and France in 2014, and how we should use the time constructively to learn the languages and learn about the culture, etc.

"What are we waiting for?" Nigel suddenly blurted out.

"Our three years to be up." I retorted, frustrated to have to say it aloud.

"We have UK passports, most of our children are in the UK, and we can live and travel anywhere in Europe. If we both think we have nothing here, why or what are we waiting for?"

"Are you for real? You would give up our Australian dream?"

As the words came out of my mouth, I realised how ridiculous they sounded. What dream? Our dream had drowned in the floodwater, with the loss of our house and our woodland. Here we were doing doggy paddle in the holding pool, until our Australian dream resurfaced. And what then, after 2014: we wouldn't be able to buy a house or get a mortgage easily, because of the bankruptcy remaining on our credit rating for seven years, so what would we really do.

"What dream? It's over. Are you happy now?" Nigel continued.

"No, but I don't want to be failure. I don't do failure."

"What constitutes failure then?"

"The UK, we left for a new life, remember?"

The conversation rattled on over several glasses of red wine, until we were both asleep on the couch.

The next day at work, I went for lunch with my good friend Anna, who is Italian in origin, to the local French pâtisserie called 'Daci & Daci.' We would sometimes visit this unassuming restaurant for a light lunch, to escape from the humdrum and politics of office life. I told her about the previous evening's conversation and about our homesickness. Anna was always honest and forthright.

"Sarah, I would be very sad to see you leave, you are a good friend but family and happiness must always come first."

The key words here being family, and happiness.

"I do not like goodbyes, and of course, if you go I will require regular updates on your new adventure, and an invitation to visit."

Our lunchtime chatter continued, as these words and many thoughts from the previous evening rattled through my head. Then it dawned on me, leaving Australia would not mean we that we had failed, it meant we were ready to move onto the next adventure that would add to the tapestry and patchwork of our life to date.

From that day on, we talked about the UK, France and Italy on almost a daily basis; we had serious decisions to make, because if we left we would not be able to afford to return anytime soon. In addition, we would need the permission of the trustee to leave, but we established with professional advice that with the balance of our family in the UK and Europe the permission would not be withheld.

However, what about Samantha, who was about to leave for Queensland with Cam? They were going to apply for a second year working holiday visa so they could travel and look for a work sponsor, as they now wanted to live in Australia. Now one of my children wanted to be here; well two really, as Jaime didn't like the thought of leaving her school friends and her social life. She had made some close friends in Hobart, in particular Holly, Mikayla and Emily. She also had a large circle of friends at the church she attended and had recently been baptized in a very emotional ceremony. This was going to be hard.

From left to right: Mikayla, Holly, Jaime and Emily

A lot of thought had to go into this, and my journal came out again. Lists of pros, and cons and considerations ensued, such as: Where would we go? What would we do for work? What about Jaime? What about the boys? They had never travelled further than interstate, although they were experienced in that now, having been in the Northern Territory, Queensland and Tasmania with all of these moves achieved by road-trip; that is some achievement for 'our boys'.

Samantha and Cam on Magnetic Island, Queensland

We knew that whatever we decided to do would affect someone or something in some way, but maybe it was time for us to be a bit selfish, for the first time in our parenting lifetime. We needed to go back to our bucket list and look at what we wanted. I knew that Samantha would be safe and well looked after with Cam. Ever since he had arrived in January, he had demonstrated how different he was to Doug. He showed his love and adoration for Samantha in so many ways and did not care who saw it. Their love is natural, easy and he makes her happy, truly happy. She had a wonderful new life ahead of her and no matter where that life took her she would always be loved by us. Jaime, however, would cause us a bit more heartache before our next chapter materialised. She randomly decided that if we went back to the UK or Europe she wanted to go and live with her 'real dad, Jack,' who she claimed she had been 'getting to know' on Facebook. The shock of this decision on her part was an enormous blow for both of us, but more so for Nigel. He had loved and treated her as his own daughter from day one of our relationship. From that point on their relationship dwindled, and powerless to help repair it, I drifted in the bad atmosphere that now existed between them. Only time and learning the truth about Jack would start the process of healing the wound she had created.

With forty thousand dollars, and the juggling balls that represent our life all up in the air, we decide its best to revert to our pros and cons list again. Over the next few weeks, we spent time, most days, looking at the list. Crossing things off, adding them on, breaking them down into short-, medium- and long-term aspirations, goals and dreams: it was a blank canvas. We had to be honest with ourselves. If we put this money in a savings account in Australia, and stayed in Tasmania, we would find reasons to dip into it, whether it was for one of the kids, or for us.

On Nigel's pros list for moving nearer to the kids was that he did not want to miss any more big events. With Clair at university, studying her children's nursing degree, her graduation was going to be a big event. She was the first of our children to go to university. Also on his long term list was being able to renovate a property again. My pros list was based around the kids. I have never given up on having some kind of relationship with Molly and all of my hopes are pinned on her maturing and realising that I have and always will love her. I too wanted us to have a family home of our own again, but I never wanted another mortgage so that seemed unlikely. As we looked into the pros and cons of different countries in Europe, we realised that the UK itself was out of the question. Firstly, because forty thousand dollars would not go far there and more importantly it would feel like failure to go back. We considered Italy, a place we have always loved and planned to visit.

Then one day Nigel said, "What are we doing, we already know where we should be going?"

Somewhat bemused and intrigued I asked, "Where then?"

"France, of course, it's where we were going to go and renovate a house in 2005 with my mum, but we gave away our dream because the time wasn't right. Well now the time is right." He paused for breath, "this is it, and it's perfect. We will be near the kids; there are cheap flights to France, ferries, Eurostar trains, Eurotunnel, from the UK. That's it!"

A eureka moment. Renovation properties were definitely cheaper in France. Access to the kids would be easy and it would be a new adventure. However, there would be sacrifices, as always. Leaving Australia meant leaving John, Samantha and Cam. Moving to Europe meant Jaime would go and seek out her biological father, my worst nightmare. But, was it time for us all to confront our demons and start a new chapter. Would we move to France without Jaime? Could I deal with Jack being back in our lives, if she went to live with him? With so many questions, and so much to consider, decision time approached.

Chapter 21
The Boomerang Effect

After months of talking and decision-making, Nigel and I had at last decided what to do with the personal injury compensation. With that decision made, we also started to come to terms with the consequences of that decision and began preparing ourselves for some big changes. Can you believe this? Because I still have to pinch myself to make sure, I am not dreaming.

Despite having made an international move before, this one felt different. Our excitement however, coexisted with a degree of guilt. I thought that our decision appeared to be a selfish act, but as Nigel reminded me, appearances can be deceptive. No-one knows the rationale to others' decision-making. It felt like going 'home,' although not in the true meaning of the word. To be able to be closer to the children, one of our main objectives, as well as pursuing a long held personal dream of buying a renovation property in South West France, was ideal.

After making the life-changing decision to leave Australia, we began counting down the days to our departure. The thrill of the adventure, the anticipation of achieving a long held dream was energising. This dream, born out of the remains of our Australian dream, was our phoenix from the ashes. With our permission to leave Australia granted by the trustee, our dream became a reality, and not a fantasy to be discussed over a glass of red wine in the garden after work. We remained confident that buying a house in France would fulfil many of our wish-list items. For example:

1. Enabling us to afford to buy a renovation property outright, with no mortgage. (As bankrupts we would not have qualified for a mortgage.)

2. We would be an hour-and-a-half flight away from the children and our extended family in the UK.

3. We would fulfil our dream of renovating a rustic cottage into the

family home that we craved, and this time it would never be taken away from us.

This move would not be without its challenges. Anyone who has ever researched or experienced an international move will appreciate that the development of lists, sub-lists and scanned folders of documents is just the beginning. Of necessity, it is a well-planned, logistical exercise, utilising all of your endurance and stamina; testing you physically and mentally. The 'easy' part would be choosing and buying the renovation property. Our research revealed that there were many available in our price range, due to the housing market slump. For now though, the task was to decide what we could justify shipping halfway around the world, as it is an expensive exercise. It is ironic that because of the flood we did not have a great deal of belongings to deliberate over. Even so, what sounds like a straightforward exercise makes you questioning the value of every item in detail, even your clothes and shoes.

Then we had 'our boys' to consider, mere babies at three-and-a-half years old. They had moved before, by being driven interstate within Australia, but this would be their first flying experience. We behaved like apprehensive parents, preparing our children for their first solo overseas adventure. The preparation for their move began before any thoughts of booking our flights and travel arrangements. There are strict international pet movement medical criteria to tackle, as well as finding a reputable pet cargo company. We needed to entrust our precious cargo to the best company available. Therefore, thorough scrutiny and research of their reputation, work practices and the travel conditions for 'our boys' became the priority. Once we had chosen our pet cargo company, Nigel liaised with them by email and telephone with our many questions about their flights, the facilities and care they would receive. With the vaccinations and rabies injections given, and their special sky crates delivered, they were ready for a gruelling thirty hours of combined flying time.

The happiness and enthusiasm from the children that we would be living nearer to them again was heart-warming. The older children had accessed great travel opportunities while visiting us in Australia, such as whale watching and visiting iconic Australian locations such as Sydney, Melbourne, Cairns, the Gold Coast and Surfers Paradise. However, the physical distance between us had been difficult to bear at times. The internet, Skype and social media fill a big gap, but the physical separation had been hard to endure on special occasions when as a family we should have been together, such as birthdays, graduations, Christmas, engagements, etc.

The daily countdown fuelled our excitement, yet the apprehension of another big move and extensive travelling hung over me. It felt like the right decision, even though we didn't know a great deal about France. We had only been there on holidays and research visits when we were investigating a move to France back in 2005 with Nigel's mum, Sheila. A different adventure awaited us now, with the simple lifestyle that we yearned for.

Samantha and Cam had left for Queensland to continue their Australian adventure in June, so for the final ten weeks in Hobart it was just the three of us again. Since Jaime had made her fateful decision of wanting to go and live with Jack, life for us changed as a family unit. Nigel and Jaime hardly spoke, and with this my excitement for our move, was muted by the incredible loss that I was going to endure. With the pressures of the move, and so much to do and think about, there was no escape from the obvious deterioration of their relationship. I feared for her physical and emotional wellbeing, in her new 'home' environment. She would be living with a stranger, because they did not know each other. However, at sixteen years old if I stopped her, I would risk losing her forever. Also, this was an opportunity for Jaime and Molly to live together as sisters. A small degree of guilt convinced me that I owed her the chance to build that relationship, even though I remained committed to my past decisions. The harsh reality was that I had to trust in the upbringing we had given her. I hoped, and prayed, harder than at any time in my life, that maybe Jack had changed, and that if not, Jaime would quickly realise the error of her ways and want to return home.

The final weeks at work for both of us were arduous. Nigel principally worked the night shifts at the casino, as we needed as much money behind us a possible. However, once word got around that he was leaving, some of the team made the work more gruelling with their demands on him. He would text me through the night saying, 'only six shifts to go,' or 'for the greater good,' our favourite motivational saying from the film 'Hot Fuzz'.

For me, the final weeks at work were a bittersweet experience. I had made some good friends in Hobart, but I was desperate to be nearer the children, and excited to start our new adventure. Of course, the management team wanted all my normal work, and more, completed before I left, as my replacement had not been recruited. However, we still found time for the final goodbyes, which were tearful, but with lots of laughs as usual. The office team had a collection and bought me a large book of photographs of Tasmania, so that I would always remember my time there. The wrapping paper was creatively made by Anna, and utilised photographs taken in the office during my time there.

Of course, we had to have several lunches before my last day, to say goodbye in style. Anna took me out for a wonderful lunch, just the two of us, in a lovely restaurant. We talked about France and Italy, and the good times to come, most of which would involve good food, fine wine and, most importantly, the children. Jenny and I parted in our own ubiquitous style, over a glass, or two, of bubbly, when everyone else had gone home. We reminisced and laughed about some of our highlights including our impromptu hen night in a local wine bar. After a boring 'works do', everyone else from the office went home early, so we pretended to be on a hen night, waiting for the party to arrive, for some free drinks! Anna and Jenny keep in touch with me on Facebook and email, and I hope they will visit us in the not too distant future. I miss those lovely ladies.

In the final run up to our big move, we cleaned and moved out of our rented house in Hobart, after 'our boys' left to start their international journey. Deja vu, we were back to where we started in

Tasmania, John's house. Here we were with three suitcases and three rucksacks, ready for our next adventure. This was a difficult time because we had endured so much emotional pain due to the loss of our house, and our Australian dream, while living with John. Our loss became a reality, as we had struggled through the bureaucratic aftermath. So returning there somehow reinforced that we were making the right decision.

The first leg of the 'boys' journey would be a domestic flight from Hobart to Melbourne. They would be kennelled there for the weekend ready for a final medical check and then transfer to the international departures area for their flights to Paris. The movement of animals is dependent on you being at the final destination to collect them before clearing customs. Although they left before us, we would get ahead of them as they stayed overnight in Melbourne. They have stayed in kennels many times before, so it was not our first time apart. However, seeing them being driven away in the pet taxi, knowing that they would be on a plane for up to thirty hours was heart breaking. I imagined putting a young child alone in a box without being able to explain why or where they were going. My imagination got the better of me until, as usual, Nigel, the voice of sensibility explained that in the dark of the freight area under the plane they would probably just sleep.

After weeks of the preparation and planning, the day finally arrived for us to leave Australia and head for our new life in France. John drove us to the airport. As we sat in Hobart Airport departure lounge drinking coffee and chatting, three of Jaime's school friends arrived to see her off. With lots of tears, teenage girl hugging and mobile phone photographs, finally the time came for the last goodbyes, before we walked to the departure gate. For Nigel, to say goodbye to John, took a lot of inner strength. It brought back the memories of our visit to the UK for our wedding, and his final goodbye to his mum, who was in the final stages of liver cancer. John had been so good to us, and was such a big part of our life, especially during our time in Tasmania. We honestly did not know when we would see him again, but knowing that he supported our decision helped us a great deal.

At Hobart Domestic Airport, you have to walk across the tarmac to board the airplane. As we walked up the steps, we could not help but take our last look around at the beautiful scenery and the departure lounge windows where John was still waving. We found our seats and a few moments of personal quietness fell upon us, amongst the hubbub of other people boarding. Brought back to our senses by the final 'take your seat' announcement we reflected on how lucky we were to have avoided paying excess baggage charges. Our heavy suitcases contained minimal clothes, but plenty of tools and essential basics for daily living on our arrival in France. Our belongings were booked to start their journey from John's house on 27th September. The courier agency 'Pack and Send' offered an efficient and straightforward service. Our thirty boxes would travel by sea freight, arriving in approximately three months, giving us time to get settled.

After a domestic flight to Melbourne, we transferred to the Etihad overnight flight to Abu Dhabi, then a connecting flight to Paris. The whole experience was quite surreal, like watching the latest episode of a reality television show. With all of the flights on time and excellent service throughout, I managed to break with my usual long-haul flight behaviour of no sleep, and managed a few hours. This I hoped would help prepare me for the ordeal, which I always hoped I would never have to face: meeting Jack and handing over my precious girl, Jaime. I still can't believe this happened

We arrived at the airport, collected our luggage and picked up the hire car. As we drove the short distance to the hotel, where we had arranged to meet Jack, the car was quiet. Tiredness and apprehension had kicked in. As we pulled into the car park, my heart was beating out of my chest when I saw him standing there, leaning against a car. Even though I had not seen him for a few years I knew it was him. Nigel pulled up alongside him and we all got out. This was a strange scenario for Jaime, because he was essentially a stranger; even though they had 'chatted' on Facebook, she did not 'know' him. For Jaime's sake Nigel made small talk, for which I was extremely grateful because I could not speak. I tried to hold back my tears as I hugged her and said goodbye. My heart was breaking just as it did when he took

Sarah Jane Butfield

Molly.

Jaime whispered, "I love you, mummy."

That was it; I could not contain my emotions anymore. I had to turn my head because the tears were falling furiously and I had promised I would not cry until she was gone. Jack ushered Jaime into the back of the car, and I left Nigel to say goodbye. I couldn't look back. I did not know when I would next see her, although we had planned to speak the following day, and she had promised to text me when they got home to the UK.

After Nigel and I checked into the hotel, we went for a walk to the small village nearby. The very essence of France existed in this small village, which had obviously been there many years before the airport descended to disrupt rural life. Industrial estate buildings for warehousing and logistics now surrounded old cottages and barns converted into restaurants. We bought two microwave dinners and a bottle of wine. I did not want to talk and there was nothing left to say. Back in our hotel room, we consumed our microwaves dinners, and settled down to watch some French television. It's great watching foreign quiz shows with jet lag, when you have no idea of the questions, let alone the answers. A long soak in the bath, followed by the remainder of the wine, made me hopeful that I could put the events of the day temporarily to the back of mind to allow sleep to envelop me. In true jetlag style, I managed only a few hours' sleep. By 3am we were both awake and drinking tea, contemplating the French bureaucracy we were soon to negotiate to secure the return of our precious 'boys.'

Jaime was always in my thoughts, and although she had texted me as planned, she was not giving much away at this stage. All I could do was to carry on with my new life, waiting and hoping that God was listening to my prayers and watching over her for me.

'Our boys' were due to arrive on Malaysian airlines at 6.40am and we had to be there to collect them from customs. My ten-week French language course at the local university in Tasmania before we'd left did little to help us understand the process. A great deal of waiting, walking from office to office, ensued. For the staff there it was just another day and we were another task for them, but for us this was a very big deal. We needed to pay the airport charges, which we couldn't even work out how much it was, and complete the vaccination paperwork for customs clearance. They were saying something about going to the warehouse with our variety of documentation from the different departments. When we got to the warehouse no-one appeared to notice us, they continued standing around drinking coffee, and talking loudly until we waved our paperwork and a man came over. One of the staff recognised a few words of my pigeon French and then we found out he spoke a small amount of English, which would have been helpful to know earlier in the process.

'Our boys' came out of the warehouse in their sky crates on a pallet on a forklift truck. With their black noses up against the grids of the sky crates, they looked so small and vulnerable. The French workers looked quite bemused as we quickly got them out of the crates, and hugged them. We put their leads on, letting them stretch their legs on a small patch of grass in the yard. We had hired a nine-seater, people carrier that was an excellent choice, because the back row of seats when moved forward left the perfect space for the two sky crates to slide into place. We could now set off on the next stage of our journey.

Vive La France – we made it. Our family unit now consisted of a man, a woman and two Australian cattle dogs. Heading off from Paris to South West France, to find their destiny and live happily ever after: well something like that. We know that despite our planning and research, this move will and does have its challenges, but 'he who dares wins' as Del boy, from the television comedy show, 'Only fools and horses' would say.

The next chapter for Jaime. After only a few weeks in the UK, Jaime was in hospital with a relapse of her CRPS. This relapse was the result of a pain in her foot after knocking her toe. Jack, however, did the one thing a parent of a child with CRPS should never do; he did not believe her. This was the beginning of the end for their relationship. After accusing her of 'making it up for attention' Jaime saw his true colours when he left her alone in hospital, something we had never done. I flew over and slept beside her in the hospital bed until she was fit to go home. We stayed at my sister Susie's for a week and against my advice, Jaime decided to give him another chance. However, just after I arrived back in France that night, I received a call to say Jack had stolen her pain medication from her, claiming she did not need it. There could be no more second chances.

"It's time to come home now, Jaime", Nigel said to a sobbing and distraught little girl on the other end of the mobile phone.

It was the final straw: my brother-in-law, Darren, collected Jaime and took her home with him, as we booked her flight to France. This signalled the end of the Jaime and Jack episode.

Our new home, renovation project and sanctuary in France

So what happened next? Nigel and I are now the proud, outright owners of a small rustic cottage in department 16, South West France. Now the real work begins. Nigel is working part-time as a labourer, as well as renovating our cottage at every opportunity. Jaime is living and working in Suffolk, studying as a British Horse Society apprentice.

Our children from around the world have visited us in France, and Nigel and I have visited them in the UK. The good life, our dream reborn, feels so good and we are the happiest we have ever been. We have very little in monetary and materialistic terms, but what we do have is ours. No debt, no credit cards, no mortgage, but all that we need to be happy, safe and positive for our future in France.

Our learning curve is huge and will continue to be so for several months, if not years to come, as we aim to integrate into the community as much as possible. A great source of information, inspiration and networking since arriving in France has been the various French forums we have joined. I am in awe of the amazing people who make transformations to their lifestyles and French properties in challenging circumstances. I have had many offers of meet ups for coffee and local information on exercise classes, markets, etc. from my new network of friends, for which I am extremely grateful.

With so many idiosyncrasies to our new life in an idyllic French village, I have to keep my journal by the kitchen window to record them. I am looking forward to sharing our French adventures with you, including: finding our new home, meeting the locals, and how our family dynamic has changed as a result of the move. There are new additions, new developments and many more tales from our large widespread family, in the sequel, titled 'Two dogs and suitcase: Clueless in Charente'.

Don't miss the bonus photographs from our time in the Northern Territory, Queensland and Tasmania at the end of this book.

About the author:

Author Sarah Jane Butfield was born in Ipswich and raised in rural Suffolk, England.

Fulfilling her childhood dream and becoming a nurse, was just the start of her amazing journey. Her nursing and teaching qualifications would take her around the world, enabling her to work in all fields of nursing, education and management. However, after 27 years as nurse, wife and mother of four children and three step-children, Sarah Jane has now achieved another long held ambition.

Glass Half Full: Our Australian adventure, her debut travel memoir, has been followed by the sequel, Two dogs and a suitcase: Clueless in Charente. The expat kitchen garden diaries – Our Frugal Summer in Charente, to accompany the sequel, is due for release later this year. In addition to writing her travel memoirs, she also works as a community manager for an online parenting community and is a published freelance magazine journalist and blogger, in the healthcare and writing arena's. Sarah Jane is currently working on a series of self-help books for people facing challenging life events and tough family situations, based on her real life experience of divorce, bereavement, child custody issues, migration, parenting, etc.

Thank you for reading.

Note from the Author:

Reviews are gold to authors! If you have enjoyed this book, please consider rating and reviewing it on the site from which you purchased your copy.

Other Books by Sarah Jane Butfield

Two dogs and a suitcase: Clueless in Charente

The title says it all: what we have and where we are. This book, the sequel to Glass Half Full: Our Australian Adventure, follows our French exploits as we endeavour to rebuild our lives in another new country, after spending four and half years in Australia. Our goal, or hope for the immediate future, is to focus positively on the present, so that we can start a new, optimistic future back in Europe. Our main aim is to be nearer to the children, leaving the dark clouds of the challenges we faced in Australia as a distant memory. Journey with us as we arrive in rural South West France; enjoy my reflections, thoughts, and observations about my family, our new surroundings, and our lifestyle. Follow the journey of my writing career and how we start our renovation project while managing our convoluted family life. Once again, we will laugh, cry, and enjoy life to the fullest with a generous helping of positive spin thrown in for good measure.

New release - coming soon: Our Frugal Summer in Charente: An expats kitchen garden journal is due for publication in Autumn 2014. A spin off from Two Dogs and a Suitcase: find out how a woman with a reputation for culinary catastrophe, kept her family fed in France with very little money, 5 chickens, 4 ducks and a vegetable garden.

To hear about Sarah Jane's latest books, author events and great competitions, sign up for Travel Memoir News -Author Sarah Jane Butfield's Mailing list. http://eepurl.com/0IuML

Bonus photographs from our time in the Northern Territory, Queensland and Tasmania

Waterhole, Ormiston gorge, NT

Ormiston Gorge, Northern Territory

Rainbow Valley, Northern Territory

The Gap- entrance to Alice Springs

Gold Coast, QLD

Brisbane CBD, QLD

Sharing our shower in the woods,
Millmerran, QLD

Our high set Queensland house before
it was submerged in the Brisbane floods

East Coast, Tasmania,
Christmas Day 2011

Marion Bay, Tasmania

Mayfield Reserve, Tasmania

Dave and Buster camping, Mayfield Reserve

My sister Susie and Darren

Father and Son – Nigel and John

Mother and daughter reunited: Sarah Jane and Molly

CPSIA information can be obtained at www.ICGtesting.com
Printed in the USA
LVOW01s2051160415

434885LV00018B/488/P